SINFUL CINEMA SERIES

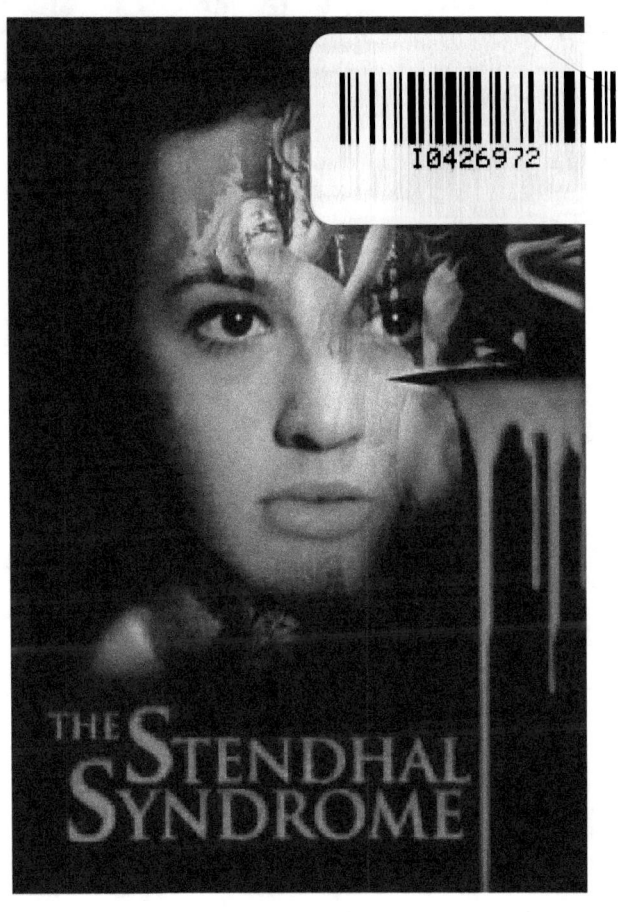

THE STENDHAL SYNDROME

Doug Brunell

SINFUL CINEMA SERIES: THE STENDHAL SYNDROME

by

Doug Brunell

©2024 Doug Brunell

Chaotic Words

Front and back cover illustration: DVD cover image

ACKNOWLEDGEMENTS

This volume would not have happened without the urging of Erin Nixon. I had picked the film to be covered for this book at random, as I always do, and then was on the fence as to whether I should choose another. I thought there had been enough written about *The Stendhal Syndrome*; it is a well-known film, and it was my favorite from the famous director Dario Argento. All those things made me want to pick another film, but then I made the mistake of telling Erin what film I had selected.

I usually keep the film I am writing about under wraps because I like to surprise people. Since I was on the fence on this one, and Erin has a way of convincing people to tell their darkest secrets, I reluctantly spilled the beans . . . but with the idea that I was probably going to choose another film. Erin hated that idea and pushed me to write about it. When I told her I thought everything had been said about Argento's movie, she countered with the fact that my perspective was not out there yet. When I said it was a popular movie, she, a film lover, admitted to never having seen it.

I am glad I decided to stick with this one. Watching it this time around with a more critical eye brought many things to light, and I think you will find them interesting, if not fascinating.

I would also like to acknowledge the incredibly knowledgeable Troy Howarth. I asked him if he would like to do an interview, and he happily agreed. I cannot thank him enough. Argento fans: this interview is a good one.

And, of course, the always-there Dayna James. Her role in all this is tougher than mine. She corrects what I screw up. Without her, this would not be the same. That said, any mistakes you find are mine and mine alone.

Thank you, all.

DEDICATION

I do not normally do dedications in this series, but I need to here. The world lost a good, one-of-a-kind man on June 16, 2022. Steven (Steve to friends) Ray Kaleookuualohapoinaole Cordero was a dear friend, whose insights and enthusiasm for film helped inspire me to write this series. He was so inspirational, that there is an acknowledgement to him in the first book in this series on *The Abductors*. Steve would have disliked the film I'm writing about in this volume. He would have found it too mean-spirited and uncomfortable. He would rather watch zombies eating people any day over maniacs wielding razor blades.

You are missed, Steve. You went too soon.

WHEN IN ROME

For those of you who follow the series, this volume's film pick may seem like a strange choice. It is not an obscure film by any means, and it is by a director who is as well-known as he is influential. It is also a newer film compared to many of the other ones I have covered so far. So why did I pick it?

Believe it or not, *The Stendhal Syndrome* was another random pick. It just so happened, however, that it was a film I had seen before. Incidentally, it is also my favorite Dario Argento movie. These things, along with it being well-known and newer, made me reconsider several times if I wanted to write about it. After all, *a lot* has been written and said about the film, and many of the people involved in it have been interviewed (and I knew my chances of securing interviews with any of the Argento clan was slim-to-none). The biggest question I had was: Could I add anything new to the discussion of this movie? If you read my acknowledgements prior to this, you know I eventually concluded that I thought I could do so. Did I, though? That is for you to decide. If I can present something new about this film, change someone's mind about it, or cause someone to watch it for the first time, then it was worth it. As it stands, this is the first *Sinful Cinema* book that is this personal. It is the first I have written about a film that means something to me. Believe it or not, that makes it harder because I want to do the film justice, and I want to remain as impartial as I have with the other films I have covered. At the same time, I also want to celebrate it and properly get across why it means so much to me. I hope I succeeded.

Now onto our feature presentation . . .

THE STENDHAL SYNDROME

Classic paintings scroll down the screen as viewers are informed that the film they are about to watch is based on the book of the same name.

Anna Manni (Asia Argento) makes her way through crowded streets. She passes by and observes old, ornate statues; a newly married couple having rice thrown at them; and throngs of tourists.

Anna ends up in an exceptionally long and crowded line of people waiting to get into the Uffizi Gallery, a prominent and historical art museum in Florence, Italy. Her eyes scan the crowd. When she finally manages to make her way into the museum, she takes in the art and looks out at the views from various windows. As she walks 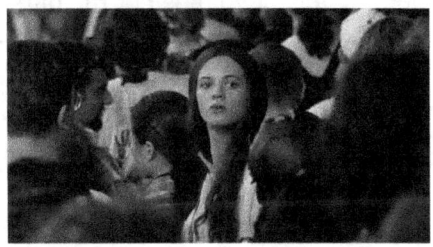 among the historical paintings, including Caravaggio's 1597 *Medusa*, she starts to hear the action depicted in the works of art around her. At one point Anna, seemingly mesmerized, reaches toward a painting, setting off an alarm. Anna's eyes dart back and forth, and she is about to faint as the "noise" of the art becomes overwhelming.

A blonde-haired and well-dressed man watches Anna from afar as she stares at a painting, *Landscape with the Fall of Icarus* by Bruegel, a portion of which shows a person falling into water.

Anna finally succumbs to the overwhelming feelings and faints, her head hitting the floor. She also drops her purse, exposing a gun inside it.

Anna finds herself underwater in the painting. She kisses a fish that approaches her and then she swims to the surface, only to regain consciousness on the museum floor as museum staff members are attending to her. One of the staff tells her it must have been the heat that caused her to faint. Her lip is bleeding from when she fell to the floor. She gets up and leaves the scene, forgetting her purse, which is shown with the gun now missing from it.

Anna goes outside the museum and sees performing street musicians dressed as vagabond-like clowns. The blonde-haired man who was watching her has followed her outside. He hands her the purse she left behind and a handkerchief for her bleeding lip. Blood has also dripped onto her white blouse. The man offers to take her to the hospital, but she declines. He introduces himself as Alfredo (Thomas Kretschmann) and asks her name. She does not answer him, but begins searching through her purse, revealing a book called *The White Knight*. She also finds a hotel room key for the Porta Rossa with room number 47 on it.

Alfredo keeps asking Anna questions as she tries to walk away from him without answering. He explains to her that great works of art have power over people (alluding to the medical condition that is the film's title), and she claims not to understand what he is talking about. She walks to a cab, and he insists upon giving her money to pay for the ride. She gets in the back of the cab and rolls up her window. She is looking out the window, with Alfredo's reflection to the left of her face. Artwork replicas are seen all around the streets as the cab drops Anna off at the Porta Rossa hotel.

As Anna walks into the hotel, the staff call out her name. The desk clerk has a message for her from Chief Inspector Manetti. Anna is still feeling out of sorts and sweating profusely. When she makes it to the room number on her key chain, she enters and empties her purse. A few of the items that spill out of it are a map of Florence, Italy and a book titled *Florence by Night*. Anna, whose name has only been spoken by the hotel desk staff at this point, obviously does not remember who she is and is distressed by that.

Anna goes to a mirror and stares at her face and says the name she heard the hotel staff say. "Manni." She then goes back to the items she dumped from her purse and finds a pill bottle. The pills are for "relaxing and sleeping," and were prescribed to Anna Manni from a doctor in Rome. Anna picks up the phone and calls the operator, asking for the phone number for an Anna Manni in Rome. When she dials the number, she hears her own voice on the outgoing greeting message and slams down the phone.

Anna takes a few of the pills and lies down. She sees a spider on the pillow and then stares at the framed print on the wall of Rembrandt's famous painting *The Night Watch*. She can hear the men in the painting talking.

Anna tries to take the print off the wall but is unable to, so she covers it in a towel instead. She is sweating again and can still hear the men talking. She uncovers the print and has a quick mental image of a man carrying a gun. The painting then melts from the wall.

There is a large hole in the wall revealed by the melted painting. Anna walks through it. Suddenly she is at a crime scene in Rome. An officer tells her that she cannot pass. She says to him, "It's okay. I'm a police officer." A plainclothes officer named Marco (Marco Leonardi) vouches for her. He wants to know where she has been, and he informs her that they found a woman an hour ago and that Manetti wants to speak to her.

Inspector Manetti (Luigi Diberti) finds her and states that the woman they found has been dead for about 12 hours. There was also another body they found, and he believes the man who did it raped 15 women, but only killed the last two. He wants Anna to go Florence because they believe the man raped three women there. Manetti says that since she has followed the case, she is the right person to send there. Manetti feels as if the man will not stop killing.

Marco and Anna walk on the street where the crime scene is located, and he says he wants to go to her place for pizza and a video. Anna's hotel room is visible through the opening in the wall. Marco is called away and Anna stands in the opening to her room and looks out at the crime scene. She then walks into her room toward her bed.

Anna turns around and sees that the print is back in place. She stares at her reflection in the glass that covers the print. Alfredo's reflection joins her own. He smiles at her and then touches her chin before throwing her onto the bed. Anna hits him, but he pulls out the gun he took from her purse and calls her "Inspector Anna Manni." He puts the gun in her mouth while running his free hand over her body.

Alfredo eventually takes the gun from her mouth and tells Anna that he knows she came to Florence to find him. He opens her blouse at her waist and tells her that he wants her the way she was earlier in the morning. He reveals that he has a razorblade in his mouth, which he flips around with his tongue.

Alfredo takes the razor from his mouth and slowly slices Anna's lower lip open. She licks at the wound. Alfredo, sweating, tells her he wanted to kiss her bleeding lips so badly at the museum, and then he does just that before raping her.

During the rape, Alfredo slaps Anna to keep her awake. She starts to pass out despite his efforts. He demands that she stay conscious so they can orgasm together, then the screen goes black.

We next see a close-up of Anna's face and hear a woman screaming. Anna stirs and realizes that Alfredo is raping another woman right next to her. The woman getting viciously raped savagely bites Alfredo's lip and he slaps her. Anna notices a snow globe that was in her hotel room. Inside it is a replica of the famous statue *David* by Michelangelo.

The other victim continues to scream. Alfredo pulls out Anna's gun and holds it near the screaming woman's cheek. He then fires it, and we see the bullet enter the cheek in slow motion where it exits the other side of her face, splattering Anna with blood. Alfredo looks at Anna through the holes in the woman's cheeks and laughs. We then realize they are all in a car as Anna gets the door open and falls out onto the street. She runs away.

Alfredo, shirtless, casually gets out of the car and aims his gun toward the running Anna. He refuses to shoot, however, allowing Anna to run further down the street as people watch from their windows.

As Anna continues to flee, a car approaches her from behind. Two policemen eventually get out and grab her. Anna screams, "No!" The police want to know what happened and want her to calm down. She identifies herself to the police and the paramedics arrive for the woman who has been shot.

The scene shifts to a crime forensics team combing through Anna's room. One officer, outside her room in the hall, finds the towel that Anna used to cover the print on her wall. Meanwhile, a doctor finishes his examination of Anna, who is talking to a female officer. The officer asks if Anna could identify Alfredo again, and Anna states she can. She asks Anna if she has seen him before. Anna says she has seen him at the police station, as the composite sketch they have of him looks just like him.

The doctor gives Anna a shot of a light sedative after apologizing for all the tests he has put her through. He also tells her not to worry about her memory loss, as that is common. After being left alone in the room, Anna grabs a pair of scissors, goes to the sink, and begins to cut her hair.

Next, we see a short-haired Anna sitting on a train. She sees her reflection in a glass of some unidentified liquid. She picks up the glass and breaks it, cutting a few of her fingers. She refuses a man's offer of help. When he asks if the cuts hurt, she simply says they sting. She smiles as her blood drips onto the white tablecloth.

When Anna reaches her destination and exits the train, we see that she is in Rome. Marco meets her and tries to kiss her. She moves away from the kiss. Undeterred, he takes her bag and asks how she is doing.

Anna is then in a room where there is a painting of a waterfall with statues on either side of it. Manetti is on his way. The painting before her melts and Anna walks into the real scene. She steps behind the waterfall.

Back in the room, Manetti arrives and tells Anna that the commissioner is waiting to talk to her. She is then sitting at a conference table surrounded by men and seems overwhelmed. Her hands are under the table, unbending a paperclip, which she then shoves under her fingernail.

Later, Anna is in Manetti's office. He gives her a new gun and a new badge. He says he feels horrible and responsible for what has happened. Anna's only reaction is to note that the gun is a 9mm. Manetti tells her that the rounds are steel-capped and instructs her to stay near the office and see the psychologist every two weeks.

Anna reminds her superior what he said about Alfredo not stopping now that he is killing women. Anna notes that he did not kill her. She realizes he wants her alive for some reason. Manetti informs her that he is giving her a twenty-four-hour police escort soon.

Anna then visits the psychologist, Dr. Cavanna (Paolo Bonacelli, from the infamous 1975 film *Salò, or the 120 Days of Sodom*). She tells him she is on the anti-rape task force. She describes getting a call in her room while in Florence from a woman who knew the identity of the rapist the task force was seeking. The anonymous caller said the rapist would visit the museum that morning. Anna explains that is why she went there, and then tells the doctor what she did in the museum and how she entered the painting. Dr. Cavanna explains to her that she has experienced Stendhal syndrome.

Marco comes to visit Anna at her place, and he has brought with him a Buster Keaton movie and a frozen pizza. He notices a bowl of chocolate candies and states that he thought Anna did not like chocolate. Anna informs him that she likes it now. Marco, unperplexed, tells her that he has missed her. She tells him that she cannot make love anymore and that she is no longer his woman. When he hugs her, she pulls away. He tells her it has been so long since they have made love. She smiles and then asks if he wants to have sex.

Anna starts to get sexually aggressive with Marco, backing him against the wall. She starts pulling at his pants and then turns him around so that he is facing the wall away from her. She starts pushing up against his buttocks and telling him that she is now fucking him. She shoves her hands down his pants, and he asks her to stop.

"Shut up," she says. She does not want to "hear his voice." She then tells him she has not finished yet. She throws him to the ground and kicks him. He leaves, and she sits at the table and eats some of the chocolate candies.

The scene cuts to Anna back in her psychologist's office. She is telling Dr. Cavanna that she wanted to have sex with Marco like a man would do it. "The idea of being fucked disgusts me," she says. She reveals that she fears what is inside her. She says she keeps cutting and hurting herself. The room is heavily shadowed as she reveals this information. When pressed, she admits to primarily hurting her hands. The pain, she says, makes her feel alive.

The doctor insists these feelings will go away soon. He then advises her to go visit her family in Viterbo. She explains that she does not want to go there and that she became a cop to escape that place.

Despite her reluctance, she returns to Viterbo and the first thing she notices is that the Museo Nazionale Etrusco di Viterbo (National Etruscan Museum) is undergoing renovations.

Giulio (Lorenzo Crespi) and a friend greet Anna. She jokes with them and then goes to see her father (John Quentin) and brothers. At dinner, one of her brothers observes her new haircut and says she looks like a boy. She leaves the table in anger and her father admonishes the young man.

Later Anna drives with her father around town. He asks if she has seen a doctor. When she says it is a psychologist she is seeing, he asks her if that is necessary. She says she thinks it is because she has "problems." They pass by the museum and her father states it has been under restoration for two years. Anna remembers being in the museum as a little girl. She recalls seeing a statue of Medusa and being overwhelmed by the art all around her.

Anna calls her doctor on the phone and reveals that her father never went to the museum. Her mother, who was a painter and read Anna fairy tales as a child, took her instead. At this point the camera tilts, placing Anna sideways in the frame as Anna states she wants to try her hand at painting and asks if this is all right. Dr. Cavanna thinks it is fine, and as he is saying this the scene changes and we see Anna's reflection in an art supply store window before we see the physical form of Anna come into frame.

Back in her room, Anna applies red paint to a white canvas. She then puts black paint on her fingers, which she uses as a brush to smear the paint onto the canvas. Then, with a brush, she starts to paint something in red that looks like a vulva. As the camera pans back, we see that she is really painting a red teardrop on a screaming face. The black she was painting is its gaping mouth and as that fills the screen, we hear the painting scream.

The scene shifts to Anna in a gym sparring with Giulio. To his surprise, she hits him in the face. The gym owner tells her to calm down before someone gets hurt. Anna hits Giulio in the face again and then walks away.

The next few scenes are odd and at first seemingly out of place in the film. There are two women in the window of a clothing store. We are seeing them from the sidewalk outside the store. One of the women is younger with long dark hair and wearing a red dress with white dots on it. The two women look out the window and see something.

Cut to Anna jogging along a shadowed path.

Next the scene cuts back to the woman in the red and white dress from the clothing store window. She is walking down the sidewalk with the camera following her from behind. She is handed a red rose from someone offscreen. She seems happy and keeps turning back to talk to whoever is following her. We cannot hear her voice. The lighting becomes darker and now we hear her telling the unseen person about how her boyfriend was in bed.

"No, I don't expect guys to be completely honest with me," she says. She then asks if she looks like someone who believes in fairy tales. Her still unseen walking partner creepily whispers something we cannot decipher, and she says she would like to kiss them, too. She says she likes kissing.

"I'm the oral type," she says as she puts her thumb on her lower lip. She then licks her lips but gets frightened by a passing motorcycle. She says there is a place nearby where she will take the person. It is where the local "whores" go. She opens a door to what looks like an abandoned warehouse. Their shadows grow large on the buildings across the street as she takes the person's hand and leads them inside. Noises that are either from sex or pain come from the room. A train is shown speeding past on tracks. The scene shifts to a man's hands around the woman's throat. She screams and he begins to choke her. He then slaps her sweating face and rapes her. He puts a gun near her head and fires. As the bullet leaves the barrel in slow motion, we see Alfredo's reflection in it.

The scene shifts to sometime after the murder. Police vehicles are at the crime scene. Marco tells Manetti that a hooker from Senegal called them. The murdered woman's body is on a mattress.

Marco goes to see Anna to let her know Alfredo has struck again. Anna says that is what he said his name was and that they do not know if he is telling the truth. Marco points out two men outside. They are her security detail. Anna makes it known she wants to contact the women Alfredo raped, and Marco wants to know why. She says she wants to learn something. Marco tells Anna he wants to see her, and she asks him what he sees.

When we next see Anna, she is calling someone on the phone. A little boy answers. Anna asks to speak to his mother. Anna now has three paintings of a screaming face that rest behind her. They start off as small canvases on the right and grow larger as they progress to the left. The one in the middle has black eyes, and the largest one on the far left has a human figure painted in the screaming face's mouth.

The mother, carrying her child, gets on the phone and Anna asks her about her rape experience. The woman will not answer her questions. The woman says she was lucky not to be murdered and does not want to think back to that time.

The scene shifts to a messy room. Anna is naked, covering herself in paint and writhing on a sheet of paper. She then curls into a fetal position.

Another woman talks about her rape experience on the phone to Anna. She compares Alfredo to her ex-husband.

Anna has dinner with her father. On the television, a news reporter is talking about people moving into smaller places in which to live.

Anna then calls a man who says that Anna only wants to talk about his wife's murder. He wants to know what his wife's final thoughts were before she died.

Back at the gym, Anna's sparring partner bloodies her nose. She likes it.

Anna goes home to her father's house and waves at the two men on security duty outside. In the house she finds a note from her father indicating that he is out to dinner with a friend and asks if she would like to join them.

Anna instead goes to her room, where she has several art prints which match the paintings that originally made her faint at the beginning of the film. She hears a woman moaning, but then her phone rings. It is Alfredo calling to say he has missed her. He quotes a passage from Graziella Magherini's book on Stendhal syndrome. Behind Anna we see Alfredo talking on a cell phone. He knocks her unconscious.

A car speeds by the security detail's car and we see that the men who were watching Anna's house have been murdered.

The next time we see Anna, she has tape over her mouth and is lying down in a large room with graffiti covering its concrete walls. Alfredo rips the tape from her mouth and lights candles. We then see that she is tied spread-eagled to a mattress. Alfredo asks if she hears the noise, which is running water. He then asks if she remembers when she was pure like water. He proceeds to rape her, demanding that she scream. She does, and he slaps her.

Anna passes out.

When she comes to, Alfredo announces that he wants to play a game. He grabs a razor blade and cuts his palm slowly, eventually leaving the blade stuck in it. He then uses that hand to stroke her face, which cuts her upper cheek.

Marco, meanwhile, is heading up a police search party for the missing Anna.

Alfredo begins to go through Anna's files, which he brought with him. He reveals to her that he disguised his voice to call and tell her that he could be found at the museum in Florence. He licks at the cut on her face and says he knows she is on his side, and he loves her. He then reveals that he has her gun. He puts the barrel of the gun against his forehead and makes a noise like that of a gun firing and then laughs. He tells her he

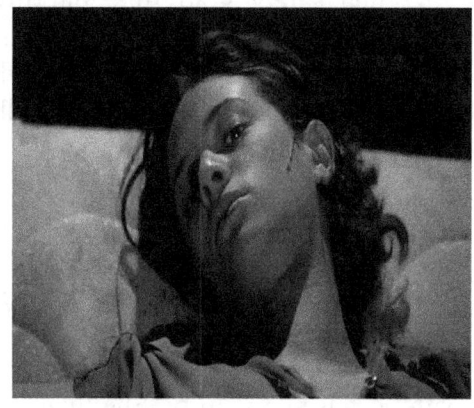

must meet someone and that he is going to rape again. He then leaves the spacious room.

Morning arrives and a bird flies into the place where Anna is being held hostage. The graffiti artwork starts to overwhelm Anna. The paintings of creatures on the walls, including a red devil with a large penis, are starting to come to life as Anna struggles against her bonds and screams for help.

Alfredo walks down some steps near a waterfall to get to his hideout. He arrives and sees Anna sleeping on the mattress where he left her. He quietly takes off his shirt and approaches her.

Anna suddenly wakes up and her arms lift, free of the bonds that held them. Each hand holds a spring from the mattress. She plunges them into either side of Alfredo's neck. She kicks at him, and he grabs her. She plunges a finger deep into his eye and gets away from him. He grabs the gun he stole from her and begins to shoot blindly.

Anna safely grabs the gun from him, and he reminds her that she is a cop and must arrest him. He surrenders to her. She shoots him in the chest and tries to do so again but is out of bullets. She then begins to beat him with the gun.

Anna tells Alfredo to move. He does not. Anna drags him outside and kicks his limp body down a path. We see signs that he is still alive, though barely conscious. Anna drags him to the top of the waterfall. She asks him if he remembers being clean. She asks if he wants to have sex. She tells him he wants to take a bath because he is dirty. She then kicks Alfredo over the edge into the waterfall.

The scene cuts to Anna and the police outside. Anna is looking at her cut face in a mirror. Marco and Manetti are consulting a map of the river. They are having a hard time locating Alfredo's body.

Marco later visits Anna in the hospital. He says Alfredo is dead. Anna says he will always come back.

Anna returns to Rome.

Back in her apartment, Anna tries on a long blonde wig, looking at herself in the mirror and eyeing her cut face. Manetti calls. He is going to see Alfredo's wife and wants Anna to come along.

Once at the house of Alfredo's wife, the woman refuses to answer any questions in front of Anna, whom she recognizes from television. Anna steps outside, but then goes back into the house through another door. She ends up in a room with art prints and

16

a statue. She finds a rolled-up print with a note stuck to it. On the note, Alfredo wrote that he wonders what effect the print would have on Anna. She then spots the snow globe of *David* that she had last seen in the car where he shot the woman through her cheeks. She shakes it.

Anna returns to Dr. Cavanna's office, her back to him as she speaks. She tells him that she is changing and that yesterday she thought her real name was Louise. She tells him of a story she just read concerning a judge on a riverbank who lends his boat to someone. The boat sinks and the man who borrowed it drowns. A man asks the judge why he did not tell the man that the boat was in bad shape. The judge replied that the question of the boat's condition was not raised. Anna reveals that she thinks Alfredo may return any minute. She can sense that he still thinks of her, wants her, and is still alive. She says she is not suffering from Stendhal syndrome. Anna also says the scar on her face will disappear after four years and two surgeries. She asks the doctor what he thinks.

Anna then finds herself at a store. She is looking at framed art print posters, as is a young man. Anna keeps slamming the metal framed posters into the man's fingers. She is wearing the wig and large sunglasses that obscure her eyes. She has a rolled art poster, and the young man states that he also studies art.

Anna drops a bag on her way out of the shop. The young man offers to carry it. Anna initially declines his offer, but then agrees to it. The man introduces himself as Marie (Julien Lambroschini). Anna says that she thought Marie was a woman's name. Marie tells her he is French, and in French it can be either. She tells him that she does not have a car and accepts a ride on his scooter. She gives him her name, and they ride off happily as he names artists he loves.

Back at Dr. Cavanna's, Anna tells him that she told Marie she was a law student. The doctor asks why she likes him. She states that Marie is not a cop. The doctor notes that she met him while looking at paintings, just like she met Alfredo. Anna just smokes her cigarette.

Anna and Marie later have a picnic with some food his mother sent to him. Marie has Anna try foie gras without revealing what it is she is eating. Anna is shocked when she finds out but likes it. She tells him that she always hated liver. Marie kisses her and exposes her facial scar. She does not kiss him back at first, but then does give him a weak kiss. The scene shifts to a fountain and people in the park as ominous music plays on the film's soundtrack.

Anna and Marie are next shown hidden behind some bushes as they kiss. A young couple shown earlier is doing the same thing, but out in the open. Anna begins to remove Marie's shirt. She wants him to stay still so she can do it herself. She finishes taking off his shirt. He starts to undo his pants, but she insists upon doing it for him. She stares at the trees above them.

The scene shifts to Marco pulling his car up next to another one. The man in the other car appears to be a police officer. He reports to Marco that Anna is home. Marco dismisses the man, telling him that he'll be on duty now.

Anna hangs an art poster in her apartment. It is now one of several that adorn her walls. Her phone rings and she answers it, but no one speaks on the other end. She looks out her window to the street below and looks around, eventually spotting Marco. She runs downstairs and out onto the street to tell Marco that someone who looks like Alfredo is down the street. Marco says he has not seen anyone like him but offers to go up to her place with her to help her relax. Anna, at this point, is dressed all in white.

Anna and Marco go to her apartment. Marco comments on all the "freaky" art posters. He then watches television. Anna is smoking in her bed. The phone rings. Anna answers and tells someone to say it is not true. She weakly calls out for Marco and is distressed, telling the person on the other end of the line not to "say that."

Anna again calls quietly for Marco, but he does not hear her. She tells the caller, "No. Leave him alone, please." She also tells the caller that "he has nothing to do with this." "No," she continues. "You better not touch him."

Anna calls for Marco again, and this time he hears her and rushes into her room. She hands Marco the phone and lies down. Marco speaks into the phone, but the line goes dead. Anna says, "It was him." Marco tells her they will tap the phone. He asks what was said. Anna tells him that the caller, whom she references as a "he" (never naming Alfredo) knows she has been with Marie. Marco asks who "she" is. Anna tells him that Marie is a boy. She says she believes "he" knows she and Marie are friends and that they make love. She says "he" is jealous and will teach Marie a lesson. Marco informs her that Alfredo does not operate that way and is not interested in men.

Anna calls Marie and leaves a message with someone to have him call her. Marco stands by listening and looking despondent. Later, he is having a cup of tea near the telephone. The phone rings and he picks up the receiver and listens. Marie is calling Anna, who has also answered the phone.

Anna needs to know that Marie is okay. When Marie says he is, Anna tells Marco to hang up. Marco ignores her and continues to listen. He hears Anna proclaim her love for Marie. At that, Marco hangs up.

Anna finds out when Marie will be finished with a project he is working on. She tells him she will meet him at the museum where he is working when he is done for the day. She tells him she wants to make love to him and then hangs up. She tells Marco she is going to take a bath. She checks something in her purse, locks the door to the bathroom, and starts to draw a bath. She then leaves out the bathroom window with her purse.

At the museum, the guard on duty tells Anna the building is closed. She tells him she is looking for Marie. The security guard says he has never heard of "her." Anna corrects the guard regarding Marie's gender. The guard does not believe her and asks who she is. Anna flashes her police ID and demands that the guard locate Marie.

Anna starts to walk the halls of the museum and finds Marie. He tells her he is done working, but just needs a few minutes to clean up. He tells her to wait downstairs, as she cannot be in the room with the art. Before she leaves him, Marie senses something is wrong. Anna admits she has not told him everything. She says she will tell him later and makes him promise to come down as soon as he is finished.

Marie goes back into the room. He is amongst large statues. Ominous music plays on the soundtrack as Marie turns out the lights in the room. Two other people who had been in the room with him leave. Marie begins to clean up, moving statues and rare artwork. Indecipherable voices play over the musical score. Does Marie hear something, or is the art affecting him, too? He calls out, "Who is it?" A gun fires.

The security guard hears the gunshot, which is followed by a second shot. He grabs his walkie talkie and gun and rushes to the room. There is blood on a statue, some smashed statues on the floor, and blood splattered on the paintings. Marie's dead body is on the floor.

Anna is smoking outside. She looks back at the museum. The guard inside the museum is calling the police. Anna sees police vehicles pull up and police run into the building. She quickly follows them in. The police try to stop her, but she pushes past them. Anna screams upon seeing Marie's body. Manetti comforts her as she cries.

The scene cuts to Anna arriving at an airport. She meets Marie's mother on the tarmac. She collapses in the woman's arms and begins crying.

Anna is awake at night in bed. She sees a butterfly on her wall. She hears footsteps. She peers out the window to see the shadow of a man on the wall outside across the street. Her doorbell rings. Anna peers back out the window and sees the shadow make its way down the street. Anna jumps back in surprise and knocks over her television, which breaks. She picks up the phone, and the doorbell rings again. Anna attempts to call Marco, but he is at the river and left his phone in his police car. The doorbell keeps ringing and is now followed by knocks on the door. Anna escapes from the apartment. She runs into the arms of Dr. Cavanna, who is out on the street. He says he needs to talk to her.

The two go into Anna's apartment to talk. Anna fears that Alfredo will never stop coming after her. Dr. Cavanna says he is the type of killer who won't stop until he is killed. He says Alfredo will be caught. Anna replies that Alfredo will never allow himself to be caught. The doctor wants to know why, and Anna says it is because he knows everything. Dr. Cavanna wants to know how that is possible.

The scene cuts to the river where a body is being pulled over it via a series of pullies and rope. The police are waiting on the riverbank for the body to reach them. An official on the scene says the body has been in the water at least three weeks. The police need to ID the body by matching it to how Alfredo was dressed when Anna kicked him over the waterfall.

Back in Anna's apartment, she is pacing around the room. She thinks Alfredo doesn't want anyone to have her, including Marie. Dr. Cavanna concludes that to mean she is Alfredo and no one else because Alfredo knows everything. Anna confirms that Alfredo knows everything about her. The doctor says Anna believes Alfredo knows her better than she knows herself. As he presses Anna on this, she demands that he leave. The phone rings. Anna's outgoing message plays and then they hear Marco leaving a message saying that they pulled Alfredo's body from the canal. He states the body has been in the water three weeks and he is afraid an imitator is on the loose. The doctor says that is no surprise. "We knew that Alfredo was dead." The doctor then says it was not Alfredo who killed Marie. Anna asks what he is getting at.

Dr. Cavanna stands up and approaches Anna, his shadow falling over her as he says it is the moment of truth and that the time has come to "shake off the lies." Anna gets scared as he approaches her.

Marco is driving and talking on his phone with Manetti. He finds out that there is no security detail at Anna's apartment and tells Manetti that she is not answering her phone. Marco is on his way to her place.

The scene shifts to Anna in her bathroom. The wig is gone. She gazes into the mirror at herself and applies mascara as the doorbell begins to ring. She ignores it. She then applies lip liner, combs her hair, and puts the wig back on. She finally answers the door. It is Marco.

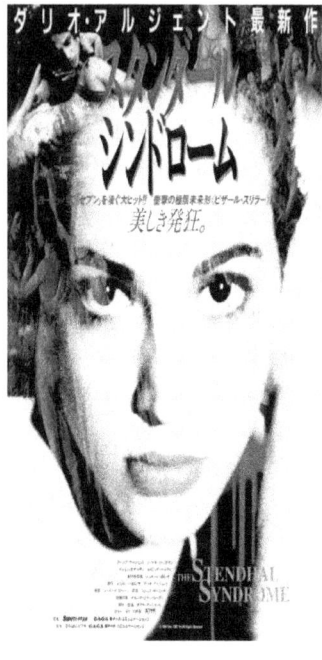

She tells him she has been home but says she did not get his message when he presses her. He tells her they discovered Alfredo's body. Her response is a simple, "So?" Marco asks Anna why she will not let him in the apartment. He looks past her and sees blood splashed throughout the room. He tries to get past her, but Anna stops him.

Marco manages to push past Anna and tells her not to move. He finds the doctor's body. Anna is now in the shadows, like a *noir* film character, with only her hair, eyes, and shoulder in the light. She tells Marco the doctor forced his way in and was saying crazy things like how he wanted to rape her. She says the doctor killed Marie. Marco asks why Anna did not call him. He does not believe her story. He thinks she has lost her sanity. She tells him the body they found is not Alfredo. She says she knows where to find Alfredo.

"He's inside me," she says. "I've become him."

Anna asks Marco why he did not realize this and help her. She admits to killing Marie. She cannot get rid of Alfredo. She says Alfredo will not stop and that he orders her to do horrible things. Marco wants to take her somewhere. She refuses. He wants her gun. She says she will lead him to it.

The two go outside to the garage. The gun is in the trunk of the car. Marco reaches for it. Anna repeatedly slams the trunk down onto the back of Marco's neck. Marco appears dead and she has blood on her white dress. She asks if he recognizes her now and tells his body that she is Alfredo. She takes off her wig.

Anna hears vehicles pulling up on the street and people shouting. She runs outside the garage, talking to herself about still being alive and needing to clean up.

The police and Manetti find Marco's body. Manetti sends the police after Anna, ordering them not to shoot her. The police eventually catch up to her on foot. The group of policemen grab her as she shouts to be freed. She falls onto the street as they try to hold her. Men's faces loom over her as they tell her they are trying to help. Anna is screaming hysterically and cannot hear them. Manetti arrives, telling her it is not her fault as she gathers her dress around her. The men cover her with a shirt as she calms somewhat. An officer lifts her and begins carrying her down the street with the other officers surrounding them.

The credits begin to roll and babbling voices fill the soundtrack.

The Stendhal Syndrome (1996, 119 minutes) divides audiences. Even among fans of director Dario Argento, it is a mixcd bag of reviews and opinions.

Before delving into a review of the film, I want to be clear that I think Argento is an amazingly talented director whose films have grown weaker over the years. I also think Asia Argento, Dario's daughter, is a fascinating person, though not always the best suited for the roles in which she has been cast. I also believe it is very hard for someone without an understanding of Dario Argento and his work to fully appreciate this film the way the director seemed to intend.

It should also be noted that there are multiple versions of this film available. Some are dubbed and some have different running times. For this book, I watched this on the Blue Underground Blu-ray limited edition set with three discs that came out in 2017. I watched it in Italian with English subtitles, which I believe is the best way to view it for reasons that will come to light later in this book. I should also state that the viewing I gave this film for my film synopsis was not the first time I had viewed it, as has been the case with many other movies I covered for this series. I had seen it at least twice prior, but this viewing only helped to solidify many of the things I felt about the film on the first viewing.

The Stendhal Syndrome is not an easy film to watch. The story itself has dream-like qualities to it that often makes the viewer question the reality of what he or she is seeing, and while the rape scenes and moments of other violence are not as graphic as they are in other films (even some of Dario Argento's other films), they take on a disturbing tone when one realizes it is a father filming his daughter in many of these scenes. If one can get past those two hurdles, however, you will find a film that combines elements of the *giallo* (Italian mystery and thriller films often revolving around a brutal killer and eroticism) and the rape revenge films of the exploitation era of American cinema. It then takes those elements and tropes and turns them against the viewer to create something that legitimately challenges both those types of film and the audience's participation in them.

The film, much like the early *gialli* made famous by Argento, is one that rewards intelligence and a careful eye to detail. In this case, knowing the titles of various classic artistic works and what they represent offers clues as to what will transpire on screen, and paying attention to the film's minor details will sometimes do the same . . . or throw you for a bit of a loop.

The Stendhal Syndrome leaves many viewers in a bit of a lurch. They feel as if the film is disjointed and wonder if maybe it was all a dream that Anna was experiencing. They feel, much like the character of Anna when she suffers from Stendhal syndrome, overwhelmed and confused by the artistic work presented. That feeling is manufactured by director Argento, and it is done purposefully. As a viewer, your focus shifts subtly throughout the film until you find yourself watching from a different narratorial point of view than you had been at the film's start without even being aware it has happened, and all of it stems from Anna.

When the audience first sees Anna, she is a face in the crowd. She is just another tourist. We know nothing about her, her job, or what she is doing. She appears as unsure of what she is looking for as are we with what we are watching. When she enters the museum, we continue mistaking her for just another tourist, albeit one who is quickly

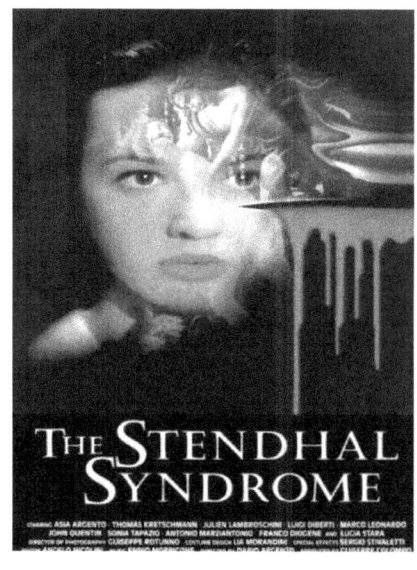

overcome by what is now commonly known as the Stendhal syndrome. MedicalNewsToday.com on November 3, 2020 published a piece by Maria Cohut, Ph.D. about the condition, noting that the term "Stendhal syndrome" was coined in 1989 by an Italian psychiatrist who named it after the pen name of the author who first wrote about it in his book *Naples and Florence: A Journey from Milan to Reggio*, which was about a journey to Italy the author took in 1817. The syndrome is noted by the feelings of unease felt in people who were witnessing the works of art in Florence. It is noted by symptoms of altered perceptions of color and sound; increased anxiety; feelings of guilt and persecution; euphoria or omnipotence; and panic attacks. It seems to only apply to foreign tourists and is only experienced when taking in the beauty of man-made art, *not* the natural beauty of nature.

Dr. Fabio Camilletti is quoted throughout the article and explains that the syndrome ties into what Freud called "the uncanny," where the experience of contexts and ideas seem familiar and unfamiliar at the same time. Dr. Camilletti states, "The Stendhal syndrome is the moment, in my opinion, where the real thing manages to filter within the boundaries of the mediatized, of the stereotype . . ." The doctor gives the example of seeing the *Mona Lisa* in person and realizing it is very real and not just something that is in pop culture.

The article also mentions a case study of a 72-year-old man who was a "creative artist." He had been having feelings of insomnia and of being followed and monitored since he had visited Florence eight years earlier.

We may not know all the effects the syndrome is having on Anna, but some are very apparent. Most notably, altered perceptions, anxiety, and fainting. Anna fainting onto her face, which causes the cut lip, is painful to watch, but it is one of the least painful moments which will torment the audience.

It is at this very point in the film where viewers need to make an unconscious but very important decision. They must ask: What is real? It is from here that the film can either be viewed as one long dream or hallucination, or as something that is really happening in the reality of the film, which is what I believe is occurring. The reality question can never fully be answered, as there are moments which follow that make viewers examine the nature of reality and dreams.

This uneasy feeling continues as the film progresses. In the beginning we watch the film from the standard narrative point of view of the audience. We are witnesses to the story much in the same way we are to most films we watch. Once Anna is raped, however, the narrative starts to slowly switch to her point of view, and as she retreats further inside herself, we are drawn more deeply into the story and start to see the scenes unfold as she would perceive and experience them. Men seem either strangely weak, such as the facial expressions Marco makes when Anna takes on a masculine sex role and simulates his rape, or they appear as predators. This can be seen most visibly at the end of the film with the faces of the policemen looming over Anna. The men who are attempting to help her, seem leering and threatening. This subtle shift in narrative point of view is sheer brilliance if you let yourself experience the film as Argento seems to want it experienced. It is vexing, however, if you watch it expecting a standard film narrative. Combine that expectation with *noir* elements, a long running time, and moments that toy with *giallo* tropes or truly make no sense, and the film can leave you either irritated or bewildered in the best of ways.

At its cinematic heart, the film is all about trauma, sex, revenge, victimhood, and the power of art. It is told through the eyes of a police officer and a serial rapist, and it takes us from witnesses to accomplices by its end, turning us into participants in unique ways. Anna and Alfredo start out as prey and predator and then switch roles after Anna frees herself from the mattress to which she is tied. A symbol of rest and the destination for lovers had become her cell, but once free she tortures Alfredo, much like he has tortured other women physically and Anna both physically and mentally. He reminds her she is a police officer and must arrest him because he *surrenders* to her. He continues to exercise power by giving her the power he has taken from her. Is it a ploy? Perhaps, but it is significant. Either way, Anna ignores her role as a police officer and continues the torture, eventually seeming to kill him by dumping him over the waterfall.

Anna was losing her sense of self before this confrontation, but at this point, she becomes something viewers of exploitation cinema are quite familiar with – she becomes revenge personified. And then the games that were hinted at with the viewer between Anna's initial introduction and her new "introduction" become the film's norms. As the Anna we know slowly disappears, so do the audience's expectations of what we thought we knew of these types of films. Instead of the catharsis we are used to experiencing in rape revenge films, we suffer a form of trauma with no relief in sight. Along with that, the familiar trappings of the *giallo* are thrown to the side, creating an even more disorienting and confusing viewing experience for knowledgeable viewers.

Dario Argento appears to be doing a poor job of keeping the audience guessing as to what is happening. Is Alfredo still alive? Is there a copycat killer? Is Dr. Cavanna committing crimes? It appears that Anna is the one behind everything from the moment of Alfredo's "death," but viewers who are familiar with Argento's work know that he likes to surprise. Viewers who are not familiar with the work of the Italian director may wonder why suspicion is even being placed upon other possibilities. It seems almost like a poor plot decision, but it is more of Argento's stylized way of keeping the dream-like atmosphere around the narrative focus. This is, of course, helped by Ennio Morricone's sensational soundtrack.

Morricone's music here is of a style called *passacaglia*, which utilizes an interesting *canone inverso* technique. Roughly translated, his score is a slow bass-filled soundtrack that uses repeated notes in ¾ time and is played the same backward and forward. It is as haunting as it is ephemeral, and it fits the mood of the film perfectly.

By the film's conclusion, the casual viewer is left uncertain of what has truly transpired. It seems like what has happened is not quite a dream, but also that it may not have all occurred as shown. For a *giallo*, it is missing key elements, such as the mystery of the killer's identity . . . unless we are to believe someone other than Anna is committing the later crimes. For a rape revenge film, it is missing the cathartic release that often comes at the end of those movies. What is left is a film that feels strangely misguided, ambiguous, and troubling. But that is only if one views the movie with an agenda of the known or with an eye that is only looking at the surface. If one watches it knowing that Argento likes to create a film that is layered, with ties to the arts, and that he is purposeful in what he presents, you start to take something very different away from the movie. What initially seems almost pointless, transforms into something radically and completely different. A rape revenge film with ties to *giallo* and *noir* blossoms into an overtly symbolic and literal examination of the transformative power of art, the lasting trauma of rape, the futility of revenge, the masculine existence, and the nature of predator and prey.

All of this is foretold in the film . . . if you understand the stories of Medusa, Icarus, and Jesus.

The Stendhal Syndrome plunges right into the land of symbolism with Caravaggio's painting of Medusa, as the story and symbolism of the mythical figure plays a very important role in Anna's transformation. Medusa's Roman-utilized story and Caravaggio's portrayal of her, in a way, foretells what Anna will become. After all, Medusa, whose tale has changed over time and is not all that familiar to people, is at her core a "living" apotropaic symbol. She is used to deter threats, though is threatening herself. Anna is much the same. Before we meet her, she is a police officer on the rape task squad charged with stopping rapists, but her role slowly becomes a threat against all men (all of which she considers threatening by a certain point) with whom she meets both casually and purposefully. Anna's transformation into her own kind of symbolic and real apotropaic symbol is reminiscent of the Roman Ovid's telling of Medusa's origin.

In Ovid's poem, *Metamorphoses*, Ovid recounts that Medusa started out as a beautiful priestess in service to the goddess Athena (also known as Minerva). Poseidon sees Medusa and is overcome by her beauty and rapes her in Athena's temple. Athena curses Medusa and turns her into the snake-haired creature much like the one we know of today. Medusa, living in exile on an island, was only visited by men who wanted to kill her, and she turned these threats to stone with her gaze. This cursed creature of "evil" was now used to ward off the evil of men. Lynn Enterline, an English professor at Vanderbilt University, has written in *The Rhetoric of the Body from Ovid to Shakespeare* (Cambridge University Press, 2000) that Athena did not curse Medusa as much as she was punishing mankind for its evil ways.

This is where the layered symbolism of Anna's transformation takes on another level that surpasses the Medusa myth. That symbolism is told in the choosing of Caravaggio's artwork.

Caravaggio's 1597 *Medusa* painting is quite unlike many other famous Medusa renditions. The artist, known for his realism, depicts Medusa's head at the moment Perseus decapitated her. The face used for Medusa is not the standard feminine face most of us are used to. It is a self-portrait of Caravaggio, a male.

The head is streaming blood from its wound, eyes wide open, with its mouth screaming. The use of Caravaggio's own face in the painting was thought to be representative of the artists' immunity to her gaze and therefore to evil. He has painted himself as the monster. In the film it represents the blend of art and violence that has changed Anna, now a creature of dangerous beauty supposedly immune to herself. Overwhelmed by art and changed by rape, Anna is not only a present-day Medusa, but is also Caravaggio's version of her. Cursed. Dangerous. Personal. Believing to be immune to her own power/curse. She has, with the assistance of trauma and (literally) art, painted herself into a monster, too.

This transformation is not noticed by Marco, who we gather was very close to Anna and wants to remain so until the end of the film, but it is noticed by her family. The same family she was at one time close to, but who drove her away and made her want to become a police officer. The family may not notice the depth of the transformation, but is aware it is there, as noted by her brother saying how Anna looks like a boy and her father realizing that something is amiss. When Marco, the man who had at one time been closest to the real Anna, learns of the transformation, he is not turned to stone but killed by Anna, nonetheless. The fate of her family is less disastrous. Her father and brothers disappear into the background, becoming less of a plot device as Anna furthers her transformation.

Marie and Dr. Cavanna are murdered as well. The threat they represent is the threat of the real Anna. The one who is not Medusa. The Anna who has been suppressed. Therefore, the threat must be eliminated. The new Anna becomes the apotropaic symbol warding off all threatening men.

The symbolism in the museum does not stop with Medusa, either. It continues with what sets the story in motion, which is Bruegel's painting, *Landscape with the Fall of Icarus*. This is the painting Anna is looking at in the beginning of the film when the Stendhal syndrome overwhelms her, causing her to faint. Alfredo is watching her, as well. The painting is not labeled in any noticeable way and what it portrays would be unknown except to someone who knows its history. It holds a major key to the ensuing story, however, and provides some excellent foreshadowing.

The Greek mythology story of Icarus is that of a boy who ignores his father's warnings and flies too close to the sun on wings made of beeswax. While that story, which is all about pride and hubris, does not seem to symbolize Anna's mental collapse, the painting does offer clues as to what will transpire.

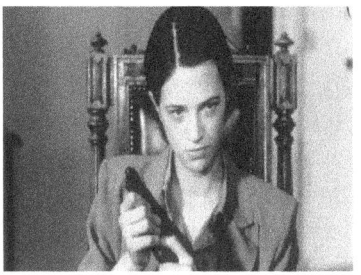

There are two key points to the painting that go beyond the mythology which concern Anna. One is the actual fate of Icarus. In the painting, and one almost must squint to see it, it is in the form of a leg sticking out of the water. It is small, and not quite central to the painting, but *nobody in the painting seems to notice it*.

The second point ties into the first as there is a farmer who is plowing the ground, oblivious to Icarus' leg splashing about. This portion of the painting is said to be inspired by a Flemish proverb which states, "And the farmer continued to plow . . .," which means that mankind is often ignorant to the plight of their fellow human's suffering. In the painting, Icarus' suffering comes from hubris, while Anna's is set into motion opportunistically, though she was initially lured into a trap of sorts.

When Anna faints, she is helped, but it is the very basic form of help. Though she hit her face, and her lip is bleeding, an ambulance is not called. In fact, it is the predator Alfredo who seems to show the most concern for her, and after watching the film we know why and understand how horrible that concern is when it comes to her well-being. The indifference in the painting is indicative of what Anna will experience after her rapes. Nobody in her life seems to take the incident all that seriously . . . except Alfredo. Manetti is the one who seems most concerned, but even he is eager to have her working again. Anna's boyfriend, Marco, barely mentions it. Anna's father acknowledges it but wonders why she needs to see a psychiatrist. Dr. Cavanna does not seem all that concerned until he pieces together what has happened. Anna, like many women who have been victims of rape, suffers alone while the farmer plows on.

The mythology of Icarus intersects with Anna, as well. Anna, who appears to be nineteen or twenty in the film, seems to be a fast-rising star of the rape task force in Rome. She was on the trail of a serial rapist, and then she fell from grace not due to her arrogance, but because of her victimization. Instead of being the person who brings in the rapists, she is now a victim of one.

The painting foreshadows Anna's fate. It is telling that while viewing the painting, she hallucinates that she dives into the same sea as Icarus, though we do not see him. We do see a fish, however, that she kisses.

In folklore, the act of kissing a fish that is caught is to give respect to the fish and to receive good luck. Anna has not caught the fish but kissing it during her hallucination could very well be Dario Argento's way of telling the viewer that the idea of good things happening to Anna from here on in are all illusionary. And that does happen to be the case. Alfredo coming to her aid and returning her bag? It seems fortunate, until one realizes that he has stolen her gun. Her regaining her identity after walking through the hole in her hotel room seems fortunate, too, until you understand that she is the very person that is supposed to solve these crimes, which reduces her avenues of assistance. Any good luck for Anna departs at this moment and never returns despite her attempts at regaining a "normal" life.

Soon after Anna faints, another bit of symbolism comes into play. It is on the street outside the museum where the recurring motif of red on white (in this case, blood on Anna's white blouse) first appears. It is a color scheme visited several times throughout the film, usually in the form of red on a white background.

Traditionally, most associate the color white with purity and red with violence, war, or strength. The Romans, however, associated the color combination with death. In *The Stendhal Syndrome*, this color combination can mean literal death, as seen in several of Alfredo's and Anna's victims, or a symbolical death as it refers to Anna's soul and personality. The latter is the more prevalent meaning in the film, and the color combination appears at so many interesting times that it cannot be coincidental.

The first time we see the red on white imagery in the museum is also when we first see Alfredo, the one responsible for destroying her soul. The color combination appears again when Anna cuts her fingers on the train. The blood on the white tablecloth here is further solidifying that Anna, who has now cut her hair and is dressing in the style of a man, has lost more of her own sense of identity so much so that she is not only taking on the appearance of a man, but is also handling her pain like a man is traditionally depicted as doing – she ignores it, telling the passenger it just stings a little. The color of the train in which she cut her fingers that is taking her to Rome where she will continue to be victimized? Red and white.

When red on white appears in the film, white is usually the predominant color. There is a notable exception, however, in the scene that involves the woman in the red dress with white dots. This scene harkens back to many scenes found in Dario Argento's other *giallo* films. The camera in this scene takes on the role of Alfredo. In other Argento films, when this type of scene is used, the audience is unaware of the killer's identity. Here it is the exact opposite, and that is partially why the color scheme is reversed. There is also another reason why red is the predominant color here, though.

The woman in this scene is set up as a victim from the start, unlike Anna. We know this woman will die. We know who will kill this woman. At this point in the film, Alfredo is still alive. There is no mystery here. In fact, the scene is almost needlessly sadistic from a psychological point of view and shows the depths of the trip on which Argento is leading his audience.

The woman acts as a seductress. In Argento's other works, as well as countless slasher films, this is what gives license to a woman's death at the hands of an unseen murderer. If only they had not been so tempting and teasing, they would be alive, or so the idea goes. In this film, however, that set up is not even needed, as we know Alfredo is the serial rapist and we have no reason not to believe it is he who is talking to her and handing her a red rose. Knowing Alfredo is the serial rapist means that this woman would be dead no matter how she chose to act. Having her act promiscuously is only meant to call forth those tropes from other films (including Argento's), which means viewers in the know will be waiting for some of the director's usual twists, such as a grisly and inventive murder.

For the astute viewers, the predominant red color in the woman's dress suggests the murder we are expecting. That expectation is almost even lustful. What makes it worse is that we are in the role of the killer here. We expect to see the woman's death happen. We can see nothing in this scene but that death, hence the abundance of red. Argento makes us complicit in it. He puts us in that role and ensures we can do nothing about it but anticipate it.

For viewers unaware of Argento's previous films, the scene only seems odd. Since we know Alfredo is the rapist and killer, why not show him? Argento eventually does, and it is in a way that is also symbolically used throughout the film.

When the woman in the red and white dress is murdered, we do not get confirmation that it is Alfredo until the bullet passes by the camera in slow motion and that is where we see Alfredo reflected in it. Those who think Anna has been dreaming this entire time may think this scene is shown from her perspective with her visualizing herself as Alfredo (a point that comes up later in the film, too), but Argento tends to use reflections here and in his other films to show the true self and the truth, even if that sight and truth is terrifying. Using the reflection in such a way here tells viewers familiar with Argento's work that he is in complete control of the narrative, and that he will take them where he wants to take them, despite them thinking they know his tricks. It also solidifies for viewers that Argento, in this scene, is placing us in the role of Alfredo. It is slow. It is deliberate. And it is

Argento, once again, skillfully manipulating audience expectations. It does not merely say, "This is a cool special effect." It says, "You are more than mere witnesses to this murder. You are accomplices. You knew where this was going, and you continued to watch. And you eagerly awaited it."

This sublime use of reflection was not the first such usage in the film, however. It is first used after Alfredo returned Anna's purse to her, though its significance was most likely not noticed at the time.

When Anna looks through her purse, we see a book called *The White Knight*, which is an obvious red herring as to Alfredo's role in her life. Alfredo is talking to her about the power that great art has over people's lives as she gets in a cab. When she raises the window, we see Alfredo reflected in the glass to the left side of her face.

The left often symbolizes a few things. It is often associated with evil. In fact, the word "sinister," comes from a Latin word that means "on the left side." To see Alfredo in this position denotes his true nature, which at this point in the film has not been revealed.

The left can also symbolize female principles and in magic, the lunar, which is also female. Having Alfredo's reflection on this side does not just speak to his personality, but also to the fact that Anna, a female, will be taking on his identity.

What is also important is the proportions of Anna's face compared to Alfredo's reflection. Having Anna's face be the main part of her we see gives the impression that Alfredo is also a part of Anna, primarily within her head, which is what Anna believes later in the film.

The use of reflections occurs in other scenes, as well, but with a bit of a different meaning each time. What is interesting to note about this scene with the cab is that the vehicle is taking her to her room at the Porta Rossa, which translated means "Red Door." It is here that Anna not only discovers who she is by going through the door of death, but also where she is first attacked by her White Knight. The symbolism is being used by Argento to both deceive and reveal, with their true nature ultimately not being understood until the climax of the film. Anna only learns of her true self by going through this door of death, but her true self is forever destroyed by walking back through another "doorway" in that same room and becoming a victim of the violence perpetrated by the White Knight, who is neither pure nor a rescuer.

The hotel staff call Anna by her name as she makes her way to her room. Looking at her reflection in the mirror, however, she tries to regain knowledge of who she is by repeating her name. She is trying to force the image she sees to become the person she is told she is all within the confines of the Porta Rossa.

Still not convinced, it takes seeing a pill bottle with her name on it, calling the phone number on it, and hearing her own voice on the outgoing greeting for reality to begin to set in. When Anna takes those pills, which are for relaxing, she sees a spider on her pillow. Symbolically, a spider on one's bed is supposed to be an omen that you are about to receive news. For Anna, this is very true, and the news she is about to receive is directly tied to the print of a famous painting she stares at on the wall. That print is of Rembrandt's famous *The Night Watch*, which depicts a group of civil guardsmen. At the time the original painting was created, the civil guardsmen were charged with protecting the city.

Anna, after experiencing more effects of the Stendhal syndrome, attempts to cover the print. It appears that this is done to drown out the noises she is hearing, but in hindsight, after knowing what her job is, it appears that she may also be trying to block out or hide her identity. She is subconsciously avoiding the danger and knowledge of what is to come, which the spider indicated was on its way. The news then comes to her in an interesting fashion.

When the print melts away, revealing a hole in the wall, Anna goes through that hole and finds herself in the middle of a crime scene in Rome that is being investigated by the police, a modern-day version of the Night Watch. Not only has she entered this scene, but she realizes she is a key part of it. This is an important scene as it solidifies her identity for herself and for viewers. She is not even identified by the other officers at first. In fact, the first one she meets does not know who she is, and she must identify herself as a police officer, which is confirmed by Marco. (Ironically, this film was made long before "toxic masculinity" was a normal topic of conversation. Anna, who ends up embodying many of toxic masculinity's traits, eventually kills Marco, who is portrayed as a weak, clueless, lovestruck male, and it is he who confirms her identity and sense of self. Dario Argento was ahead of his time with his take on the male ego.) This is followed by a bit of exposition where Manetti explains to the viewers through a discussion with Anna that a serial rapist turned killer is on the loose and that Anna must go to Florence because they believe the criminal has struck there recently.

The news Anna has received is confirmation of her identity and that she is thought of highly enough in her department, which appears to be all men, that she can go to Florence to obtain information on the serial rapist. This is news to the audience, too. The fact that she enters the crime scene through the print that depicts the past era version of the police can also be an indicator, if one was inclined to believe so, that everything she is experiencing is merely a dream of one sort or another. The more plausible explanation is that the print sparked her memory and she just hallucinated validation of it through the ongoing suffering of Stendhal syndrome.

All of that is key to establishing Anna's character, but there is one other important element to the scene that foreshadows things to come.

As Anna and Marco walk along the street, we see a blue and white sign. The sign reads, "Senso Unico," which translates to "One Way Street." Anna's Porta Rossa room is visible through a hole in the wall. The Porta Rossa hotel is in Florence, while the crime scene is in Rome. This sign symbolizes Anna's fate. It shows that Anna, by being sent to Florence, was heading down a path that could only go one way as far as her fate goes.

When Anna first gets to her hotel room through the Red Door, she is trying to figure out who she is. When she goes through the hole left in the wall by the melted print, she has regained her memory of self and her mission. When she goes back through that hole into reality of the "now," that reality becomes a living Hell.

When Anna is back in her room, she is looking at the print when Alfredo's reflection appears in the glass covering it. Audiences at this point are not sure if this is another hallucination, or even why he is there, though they may have ascertained this is the criminal she is seeking. Argento, unlike in his other films, does not make the main antagonist's identity a mystery.

This reflection of Alfredo may feel like another one of Anna's hallucinations at first, but Argento again uses the reflection to signify truth. Alfredo *is* in the room, apparently gaining entrance while Anna was hallucinating that she was back in Rome.

Alfredo's first attack on Anna is full of significance. He tells her what he is desiring, which gives insight into his mindset. He wants her as he saw her in the museum, only instead of being overwhelmed by the power of art, it seems he wants her overwhelmed by the power of his blood lust. He even goes so far as to slice her lip with a razor blade just to replicate her injury at the museum. He then kisses her to taste her blood, like a vampire. He not only wants her to feel his power, but he wants to steal her power as well and make her his subject. When he saw her succumb to the power of art in such a pure way, literally overwhelmed by its beauty, he, a man who thrives on power, wanted her to have the same reaction to him. A pure reaction to pure power and lust.

Alfredo is a serial rapist who will not stop until his mere presence inspires such a reaction. That is when he will have complete control, and when that does not work, he will resort to force. He wants to break Anna both physically and mentally, understanding that doing so will put her in the state he seeks.

Viewers are forewarned, however, as to what is to come, though they are probably not aware of it at the time even if they understand the symbolism of the snow globe with its replica of *David* by Michelangelo, which is seen in Anna's room.

The snow globe on its own represents innocence and purity. It is a child's trinket, after all. The fact that it has a replica of *David* in it is telling when one knows the history of the statue.

The statue, many people believe, depicts David right before his fight with Goliath. The symbolism there needs no explanation, but the statue does represent something else, as well.

David was meant to serve not only as a symbol of strength and defense to the people of Florence, where it rested, but also as a warning to Rome. Florence at the time of the statue's creation was having its sovereignty threatened on all sides by other states and the House of Medici. *David* faced Rome as a warning to the Medici family, as that was where they lived.

The inclusion of *David* in the snow globe is letting viewers know that Anna's purity is threatened, and that Rome is where the threat will be strongest. Why Rome and not Florence where the first attack takes place, which would seem to make more sense? Rome is where Anna not only ramps up her violence but comes to admit that Alfredo is inside her and suffers a complete mental break from reality at the end of the film. It is not necessarily a warning to Anna, but to those around her.

The camera notices the snow globe when it is first in Anna's Porta Rossa room. Anna only really notices it when she is prone in the car and the other woman victim is being raped beside her in a very grisly scene. In this sequence, Alfredo is depicted as someone who is not only physically sadistic but mentally sadistic, as well. It seems clearer in hindsight than it does during the scene, but Alfredo is toying with Anna and wants her alive so that he can experience her purity repeatedly. If he can have her as she was in the museum, forgetting all sense of self, it is like having a fresh victim every time in the same person.

While Alfredo is raping the other victim in the car, Anna regains consciousness and sees the snow globe. It becomes her focal point for a moment. This moment serves as a warning to the audience that she is under a more dire threat than it first appears. Alfredo has taken her and the one object from her room with a link to childhood and placed them in his car, where he, fresh from raping Anna, is doing the same to another woman . . . and he wants Anna to *watch*. Alfredo enjoys being the focus of Anna's attention almost as if she is a little girl watching her father work, which harkens to the actress and director's real-life relationship, as she is literally in his work in this case. It is a subtle nuance that I have never seen brought up in the criticisms of Dario Argento casting his daughter in this role, but it seems so on-the-mark that it is hard to imagine people missing it.

Alfredo takes pride in taunting Anna, as well. When he smiles and laughs at Anna through the hole he shot in the woman's face, he does it knowing the mental effect that would have on a person. When Anna flees, he purposely does not take a shot at her with the gun because he wants to keep her alive for future torments. The threat to her purity both physical and mental has now been established to be more than temporary; it is to be ongoing and everlasting.

Before heading back to Rome, however, Anna needs to go to the hospital. It is here where she will be examined by doctors and, more importantly, where she will start her transformation.

After Anna escapes Alfredo, her interactions with the police and the doctor at the hospital are far from sympathetic. She is treated as just another statistic. Another victim. This is an all-too-common treatment of rape victims by males who are investigating and "helping." The doctor is very dismissive of what she has been through. Once he leaves, Anna grabs a pair of scissors and cuts her hair short, giving her a more traditionally masculine appearance.

When Anna is next on the train to Rome, she is looking at her reflection in a glass of what may be wine. This is Anna, now with the short hair and dressed more masculine, seeing herself as she believes herself to be. She is handling her trauma as the stereotypical man would, though going about it in a traditionally feminine way. First, she cut her hair and changed her style of dress. Next, she takes to a form of cutting.

Anna breaks the glass in her hand and does not seem to react at all to the pain, internalizing it much like a man would. It is seemingly intentional that she has not cut one of her limbs with a razor blade, Alfredo's device of choice. In her mind, escaping what he has done means taking on masculine characteristics. Her personal changes do nothing to accentuate her feminine self and do everything to bring out the masculine portion of her personality. Cutting her hand is done in public, where most females who resort to cutting do so in private. It is also seemingly done "accidentally," where females traditionally do it deliberately and with ritual. This is Anna displaying her masculine strength and her veering away from her femininity. This is her starting to embrace the meaning of her surname Manni, which translates to a fierce or strong man. She is enduring the pain for another male witness and turns down his offer to help. When he asks if it hurts, she replies that it stings a little and then smiles as red drops of blood fall onto the white tablecloth. Had the witness known what Anna had just gone through, his surprised reaction may have been a bit different.

Anna is having an internal struggle, and the portion of her personality she believes to be Alfredo is winning, though she is unaware of this being an issue at this point. When she steps off the train, Marco tries to kiss her, but she moves away from him. Neither side of her personality wants to submit to Marco's quaint greeting. The female aspect of her wants nothing to do with love and physical displays of it at that moment. The male portion of her wants nothing to do with kissing another man. That will change, however, as the two sides ebb and flow in their desire to take final control of the physical vessel of Anna.

When Anna next experiences Stendhal syndrome with the painting of the waterfall, she is trying to cleanse her soul. She walks into the painting and into the waterfall. What her character knows that viewers are unaware of is that a committee of men await to talk to her. Her dealings with men trying to "help" have so far been fruitless. By walking through the waterfall and going behind it, she is trying to cleanse herself, to purify herself, to purge the victim and become the victor. She knows she will need strength to survive in her male-dominated profession and to survive the committee. Being part of the rape task force and then becoming a victim of rape changes the dynamic within the task force, something of which she is keenly aware. She may be young and a well-respected officer of the law, but now she is also a victim of something she was tasked with preventing. Anna needs to regain her strength and purity of self to not only succeed at her job, but also to stop Alfredo. Unfortunately, her meeting with the committee proves to be another setback.

Sitting at the table surrounded by the leering faces of older men proves to be overwhelming to Anna. On the surface, she is barely keeping her composure. Under the table, out of anyone's sight, her attempts to regain control of the situation come to light to viewers.

Anna's fingers work at unbending a paperclip, something we have all done at one time or another. Usually this is done when bored or fidgeting, which does not appear to be the state Anna is in. What she does next with it, though, is something most people would not dream of doing. Anna takes the end of the paperclip and shoves it under her fingernail, again internalizing pain. The cleansing waters did not help her. She now believes in the power of pain. Physical pain, induced by the unwinding of an object used to hold things together, is how she endures the mental pain and the realization that everything is falling apart.

This masculine personality transformation even carries over into her interaction with Manetti, whose surname means the same as Manni and is seemingly the only male who is truly compassionate about her plight. When he sympathizes and gives her a new gun, Anna's only reaction is decidedly male. She notes that it is a 9mm. She does not thank Manetti for his concern, and she does not react to being told to go see a psychiatrist or having a security detail dispatched outside her house. Viewers get the feeling that she does not care about these things.

Anna's first visit with Dr. Cavanna is extremely revealing as to her personality change, as well. She tells the male doctor of her work with the rape task force, what led her to Florence, and her suffering from Stendhal syndrome. She does not go into the actual rape, which is the reason she is there. Subsequent visits have her avoiding much of that, as well, though with each visit we sense more of her personality is unraveling and changing.

Even though Anna does not reveal much, a future scene with the doctor indicates it may be because she feels as if he is not asking the right questions . . . and nor is anyone else. The scene is where Anna finally reveals that she feels as if she is changing and thought her name was Louise. She tells the doctor the story about the judge and the boat and how nobody inquired about the condition of the boat before it sank. The symbolism here is so obvious as to not need comment, but it is worth noting that Dr. Cavanna should be realizing what is happening to Anna. He is, but the movie is now from Anna's point of view, and she does not believe he is comprehending her situation. Anna is telling him that she believes she is changing, but she also notes that she believes she can get better and that her physical scar will go away in time, which indicates she also hopes she will fully recover.

Before that recovery can occur, however, Anna's turn to masculinity becomes dangerous and alarming. The one who first experiences this is Marco, the man she was in a relationship with before the film's story began.

Anna's relationship with Marco from the moment she gets off the train in Rome is one of torment for Marco both mentally and physically. Marco may be the stereotypical boyfriend who does not want to acknowledge that his girlfriend was raped for reasons of it being uncomfortable for him, but as the boyfriend to someone on the rape task force and as a fellow law enforcement officer, he should have a better understanding of Anna's situation. Her treatment of him, however, is what needs to be examined so one can understand how she views herself at this point.

Marco understands Anna has changed. Her refusal to hug him at the train station and her new love of chocolates are two signs. When Anna tells him that she cannot make love to him anymore and that she is no longer his "woman," Marco should be understanding. Marco is ignorant of this, though, and instead keeps pressing Anna to make love. Her reaction to his continued pressure sets off an alarm to viewers, and it should do the same to Marco, though he ignores it.

Anna takes his advances with a smile and then asks if he wants to have "sex." Just moments before she was saying "make love," and now it is the more traditionally masculine "have sex." When she spins him around and pushes him face first into the wall and then begins thrusting at him from behind it is a decidedly male act. As noted previously, Marco's reactions to this are a bit dramatic, but that is because we are seeing it through Anna's eyes, and that is how she would *like* him to react. When she tells him that she is now fucking him and starts to reach down his pants, Marco demands she stop. She tells him to "shut up" and that she does not want to hear his voice. As if that were not enough, she tells him she is not finished yet and throws him to the ground and kicks him. When he finally gets away from her and leaves, she sits and eats chocolate.

Marco's later reactions to Anna and his continued emotional bond to her give credence to the idea that the entire event may have never happened, and it was all in Anna's fractured imagination. I would contend that the scene did happen, however, and the fact that Marco comes back to her is proof of his cluelessness to her mental state and indicative of his love for her. That love is put to the test when she calls Marie while Marco is in the apartment.

The telephone call Anna makes to Marie while Marco eavesdrops is emotionally tragic for Marco. While Anna has made it clear to Marco that she cannot love him, she also is very clear that she now loves Marie and wants to do with him what she will not let Marco do with her. Marco, of course, does not understand the implications of all of this, which will be explored further on, but he does understand the hurt it causes him. He is finally realizing that the Anna he knew and loved no longer exists, though there are signs we shall get to that demonstrate she was attempting to bring that Anna back. What speaks to Marco's character is that he decides to continue to care for Anna despite her intentionally hurting him.

The only other character aware of Anna's feelings toward Marco is Dr. Cavanna. After her sexual encounter with Marco, she reveals to the doctor what she could never tell Marco, and it places Anna's personality in a disturbing light.

Anna tells Dr. Cavanna that she wanted to "fuck" Marco like a man would and reveals that she is "disgusted" by the idea of being "fucked." She then tells the doctor that she fears what is inside her. And how is she dealing with that fear? She 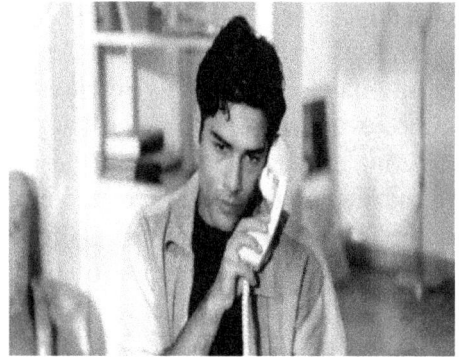 explains that she is cutting and hurting herself. As she explains this, the room they are sitting in is shown to be heavily shadowed, as the film is taking an even darker turn. It is also foreshadowing the *noir* elements that will be coming to light soon as Anna's personality undergoes yet another change.

The doctor presses her about the self-inflicted pain, and she reveals that she is primarily hurting her hands. This is significant. Though she says the pain makes her feel alive, most females will cut their limbs in a place that can be hidden from view. Anna targets her hands. Why? She is trying to stop them from acting on her behalf. Her mind may be calling the shots, but her hands are carrying out the orders. She subconsciously knows what is happening to her, and she is trying to prevent that from going its full course.

The doctor dismisses her by telling her these feelings will go away and suggests she goes back to her family in Viterbo.

Viterbo represents Anna's past, and from what we can gather, it was not a particularly pleasant one. She states she became a police officer to escape Viterbo and, one would imagine, her family. Her reluctance to go back there is overpowered by her need to heal, however, so she agrees to the visit. She is hoping to reconnect with that part of her soul she is losing.

It is telling that the first thing we as the audience notice when she returns to Viterbo is the Museo Nazionale Etrusco di Viterbo which is under renovation . . . just like Anna. The museum, as we learn in a flashback, holds memories for Anna. It was here as a child that she had her first experience with Stendhal syndrome.

Before the museum flashback happens, however, Anna is at the dinner table with her brothers and father. Noticeably absent is her mother. When one of her brothers points out that Anna now looks like a boy, Anna gets mad and leaves the table. Anna's father scolds the young man, but he is also not sympathetic to her plight.

When Anna and her father are driving around town he asks if she has seen a doctor. Anna reveals she is seeing a psychiatrist, and her father asks why that is necessary. She can only tell him it is because she thinks she has "problems." Then they see the museum and the flashback occurs.

When Anna calls her doctor after the flashback, she tells him that her father never went to the museum, but her mother did. Her mother was also a painter who told her fairy tales. At this point the camera tilts until Anna is sideways in the frame as she reveals she wants to try painting and asks the doctor if he thinks that would be all right. The sideways tilt of the camera indicates it is anything but that. Here, as in many films, it indicates an imbalance of the character.

As the doctor states that he thinks it would be fine for her to try that, the scene shifts to an art supply store where Anna's reflection is visible in the window before we see her physical form. This subtle difference from how we have seen reflections utilized prior in the film indicates that this is another, larger breaking point for Anna's personality and it is another place where the audience is drawn deeper into Anna's narrative perspective. For one instant, we, the audience, are reflecting Anna's form on the window. It is also a bit of foreshadowing for the upcoming scene where we see Alfredo's reflection in the bullet.

In both scenes we are sure of who we are seeing in the scenes before the person is revealed. In Anna's scene she has just talked about taking up painting, and we see an art supply store window. In Alfredo's scene, we are fairly confident we are looking through the killer's eyes as he follows the woman in the red and white dress. A killer we know to be Alfredo at this point. When we see his reflection in the bullet, we realize we are correct, though we have not seen his physical body at this point in the scene.

Both characters' physical selves are absent from these scenes in a way that not only places us as the characters, but also signifies the beginning of their demises. In Anna's case, her near total mental demise and in Alfredo's, his impending physical demise. Anna's mental collapse began after experiencing the Stendhal syndrome and exciting something in Alfredo, who treats her differently than he does his other victims. Art has acted as the catalyst, and now, as she actively pursues art on her own, her downfall will be hastened. Alfredo's eventual death does not really begin when Anna stabs him in either side of the throat. It is when he surrenders to her as the police officer and Anna, no longer behaving like a police officer, shoots him. This is where he realizes he may die. He is surprised by the shooting and her attempt to continue shooting him. The bullet his reflection is seen in partly symbolizes the start and instrument of his death. In a sense it is the opposite of the myth of the vampire not reflecting in a mirror because he is dead. Here the living reflect in the symbols of their demise without being "present" in the scene. The death objects take on their persona and reflect it outward.

When Anna is first shown painting, she is applying red paint to a white canvas. Prior to this, the red on white motif has usually been her blood on a white blouse or tablecloth. Pain caused by art, Alfredo, or herself. Here, as a form of therapy, she is transferring the pain to the canvas via painting what is eventually revealed to be a screaming face. In a future scene, where Anna is first trying to connect with a victim of Alfredo, we see that she has three paintings of screaming faces, with the biggest one having a small person in its gaping mouth.

These three paintings represent three stages of Anna's personal transformation. The first is her as we see her before she experiences Stendhal syndrome at the beginning of the film. The second painting, which is slightly larger than the first, is after her rape where she starts to take on masculine qualities, and we see the world through her eyes. The third and largest painting represents when she dons the blonde wig and becomes the *femme fatale*. The figure inside its mouth is the real Anna trying to come out. It only gets as far as her words with Dr. Cavanna, however, before the *femme fatale* ends up killing the doctor and Marco, and Anna's mental state totally unravels.

Anna's attempts at art therapy with the three paintings fail her, but they are an indication to the audience of what is transpiring, though that may not be apparent yet.

It is illuminating that we see the three paintings in their full state when Anna is calling one of Alfredo's victims. Anna is trying to realize what she is going through by questioning the woman and attempting to understand her and therefore understand herself. The woman's answers to Anna's questions, however, are as generic as they come. They are of so little help to Anna that it is not surprising to see what happens next when Anna attempts to paint.

Anna's art therapy and desire to comprehend her own mental state by talking to the victims are all

60

understandable and usually excellent forms of therapy. Connecting with yourself and others who have had similar experiences can lead to some sort of revelation that helps one deal with trauma. In Anna's case, however, it all seems to fail. She is not getting the answers she needs either from herself or the first victim she calls, so she decides to fully submerge herself in art and harness its power to gain insight.

Anna is shown naked, on a large sheet of paper covered in paint that she is smearing over her body. She is no longer painting but has become the painting, only it is in no discernible form. It is chaotic, a jumbled mess of muted colors, much like her mental state is a hurricane of emotions, with anger being the most prevalent. She curls into the fetal position at the end of the scene. She has regressed to become reborn. When we next see her, she is talking to yet another victim, but this time we know it is different. Anna has withdrawn deeper inside herself and will instead become the violence she has endured, much like she became the art. This concept is oddly solidified the next time Anna has dinner with her family.

When Anna has dinner with her family after her experience painting herself, the only other person at the table is her father. Her brothers are not in the picture. What is unusual about the scene is what is transpiring on the television on the counter. It is not a news story about the serial rapist, as one would expect to see in any other film. Instead, it is a story about how younger people are deciding to move into smaller places than in the past. The audience's attention is drawn to this news story. The story itself is not supposed to be a reference to Anna's physical space that she inhabits, but her mental place instead. She is withdrawing deeper inside herself, and we and her father are supposed to notice. Her father does notice, which is why he later invites her out to dinner with he and his friend to draw her out of her shell. She is never shown going to that dinner, however. She does not need to go. She has embraced what she has become, as noticed next time she spars.

In Anna's next round of sparring, she bloodies the nose of her sparring partner and likes it, another moment of foreshadowing of what is to come to Alfredo and any other man who gets near her. She finally feels comfortable with this transformation into the more masculine self, as exemplified by her waving to her security detail, which she ignored before. She can be friendly to them because she does not need them, and it helps hide what she has become.

Alfredo makes his next appearance that same night, after murdering the two police officers outside of where Anna is staying. His appearance is another moment that can strengthen the argument of those who think the story is occurring in Anna's head. He appears in her room, after he reads her passages from the real book on the Stendhal syndrome and abducting her just after she experiences the syndrome once again.

On the surface, this assumption of her imagining her plight seems valid enough, but Dario Argento's clues have said otherwise all along, and if it were in her head, her subsequent stabbing, shooting, and torturing of Alfredo should have been enough to cleanse her mind and bring her back to a somewhat normal level of sanity. After all, she uses the same kind of phrasing as he did and exhibits the same kind of sadism before disposing of him off the side of the waterfall. She has become him, but only after experiencing one more bout of Stendhal syndrome that this time features the paintings in Alfredo's hideout, including one of a devil-like creature with a large phallus, springing to life. She has snapped, and this time it is she who traps Alfredo.

As an interesting aside, right before Anna experiences Stendhal syndrome in Alfredo's lair, a bird flies into the building. It is a peaceful moment before all hell breaks loose, and it symbolizes two things, one of which happens in the future.

The most immediate symbolism represented by the bird is fate. In film, birds often represent fate and destiny. Anna's destiny, as anyone paying attention would agree with, is to kill Alfredo. She is about to carry this out, but must fully lose herself first, which she does.

The second thing the bird seems to tease at is Alfred Hitchcock, director of *The Birds* (1963). Argento is a fan of Hitchcock, and Anna's later transformation into that of the *femme fatale* is directly related to the ones Hitchcock perfected in his films.

Though Anna kills Alfredo, he has left her mentally broken and with a physical reminder in the form of a slash on her face. She is examining this cut in a mirror while the police search the river for

Alfredo's body. When Marco later visits Anna in the hospital, he tells her Alfredo is dead, but Anna coldly says he will be back. She knows this because she believes he is now inside her, and then she returns to Rome, where the statue of *David* served as a warning of things to come.

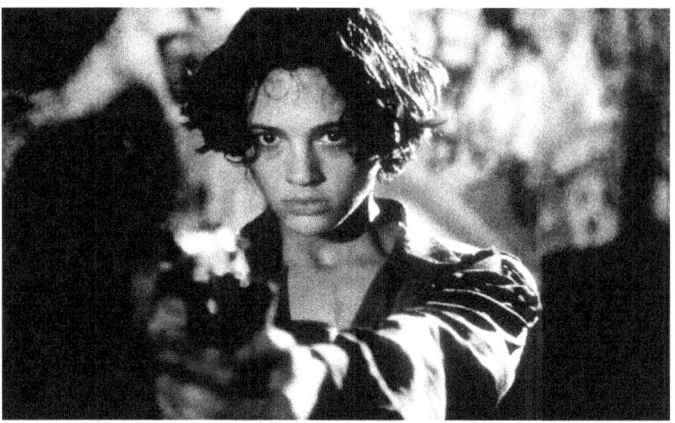

Once back in Rome, Anna begins the next stage of her transformation. This is done, again, in front of a mirror, indicating that this is who she is now. She dons a long blonde wig that is the same color as Alfredo's hair, though far more feminine, and examines the scar on her face. Anna is becoming the *femme fatale* of the film, as solidified when Manetti and Anna make a visit to Alfredo's wife.

If we were not alerted to Anna's new *femme fatale* persona when she donned the wig, we become very aware of it once we see her interact with Alfredo's wife. Alfredo's wife does not look at Anna as a victim, but as the "other woman." She will not answer questions while Anna is in the room. Why? Because she understands that Anna was more than a victim to Alfredo. It was not the rapes disrupting their domestic lives. It was Alfredo's obsession with Anna.

Anna leaves the room but sneaks back into the house. She finds what appears to be Alfredo's study and discovers a note he wrote about her wondering how the art print would affect her. She also finds the *David* snow globe that he took from her room. Anna, far from experiencing any kind of distress upon seeing this object, instead shakes it. She is now in control, and for a *femme fatale* with masculine traits, this will translate into danger to those around her . . . especially Marie.

When Anna first encounters Marie, she is wearing the blonde wig and glasses, and she finds him while they are both looking at framed art prints on a display stand. Anna keeps banging the metal frames into his fingers, which is reminiscent of how a little boy would let a little girl know he is interested in her while they are in elementary school. Under other circumstances it may be a gesture that is looked at as cute but knowing Anna's state of mind, we know this action is anything but adorable. It seems calculated to get Marie's attention, which it does.

The inclusion of Marie is no small part of the film. It begins with Anna capturing his attention and ends in his death, with every move Anna makes along the way leading to that outcome. Their dynamic is well worth exploring, and it all starts with the male character's name and what it signifies.

Marie, as noted by Anna, is typically a female name, though since he is French it can be both male and female, much like Anna's current mental state when she meets him. Marie is decidedly male in the film, but Anna gives him the traditionally female role in the relationship when it comes to sex. Even though she is now in the *femme fatale* aspect of her outward appearance and surface-level personality, she has that masculine side hiding behind the classic trappings of femininity. She started out a woman, who then took on a masculine appearance and mannerisms after her rape. After her revenge against Alfredo, she keeps some of those masculine aspects but becomes an even bolder combination of her feminine side and her masculine aspects as she believes Alfredo has manifested himself inside her. The blonde wig and large sunglasses are meant to accentuate the feminine while hiding the masculine. When she "opens" up to Marie about herself, it is all lies, and their lovemaking in the park is hidden behind bushes, where she is also the aggressor.

The only times her relationship was not hidden with Marie, whom I believe she knew she was going to kill from the moment he recognized her advances, was when she was talking to Marco and when she met Marie's mother at the airport after her son's death. Talking to Marco about Marie and letting him overhear her conversation with him was calculated to hurt Marco, but it also meant something else that is not as apparent at first. To understand that, though, one must consider the significance of the *foie gras* scene.

When Anna and Marie picnic in the park, they are eating food Marie's mother has sent. Neither Anna nor Marie has fixed the meal, which is traditionally the female's role. Anna has not done so because her only truly female aspect at this point is her disguised appearance and surface sexuality. Marie, despite taking on the female role, has only really done so in Anna's mind and when she initiates sexual contact.

The fact that Marie initially tricks Anna into eating the liver dish seems almost like it should be reversed. The dish itself is made by force feeding a duck or goose. Anna is feeding Marie lies and tricking him to turn him into a victim, much like the force-fed animal. This scene takes on a new meaning, though, when Anna admits she always hated liver but likes the *foie gras*. In the past, she has hated lying and trickery; perhaps those things being part of the reason she became a police officer. Now she likes them because she has become trickery and lies personified. She has changed, and this is a warning to Marie, much like her scenes with Marco are a cry for help masked by trickery and lies so that she can regain control of the old Anna and be stopped.

Anna bluntly tells Marco that she is seeing Marie and loves him. It is understandable that the *femme fatale* would use another man, especially a "feminine" man, to hurt her past lover. Marco is, indeed, hurt by the revelation but remains a dutiful protector of her in part because he still loves her, and because he is a police officer assigned to her protection duty. When he overhears Anna's worried discussion with Marie, something she knows he is listening in on, the emotional wounds are accentuated. What happens next is either the most careless scene in the film or one of the most subtle and important depending on how you look at it.

Anna tells Marco she is going to take a bath. She locks herself in the bathroom and escapes out the window, but not before turning on the water in the tub. This scene has only been mentioned in a few reviews of the film I have read or watched, and when it is, it is presented as a mistake on Dario Argento's behalf. I would counter that it is something else entirely.

Those who believe that Anna has been imagining everything since her bout with Stendhal syndrome as an adult could point to this scene as an indicator of that. Why would she secretly exit, but leave the tub running? The people who believe the film is taking place in Anna's head could say it was left running because her imagination has not grasped the problem with doing so, and since all that has occurred in the film is in her head, it does not really matter. I, as stated prior, believe the incidents in the film have happened, and this scene is her final cry for help from one of the few people she knows will rescue her despite the lies, trickery, and abuse – Marco.

I contend that Anna purposely left the tub running, though she did it subconsciously. It was the last part of the old Anna in Anna's personality coming to the forefront to turn on that tub. After all, she could have let the tub fill, turn off the water and then sneaked out, being sure to be quiet since the lack of sound of the water running would not mask the sound of her leaving. Instead, she leaves it running and then escapes. The remnants of Anna's original personality knew that by doing so the tub would eventually overflow causing Marco to check on her, and once he realized she was gone, he would go looking for her and hopefully stop her before she killed Marie. The old Anna did not want Marie to die. The new *femme fatale* Anna knows he will. In the end we do not know how Marco reacted or the outcome of the tub issue, but it does not matter. Marie is dead, and Anna has fully crossed the line. Or has she? Dario Argento has one more trick up his sleeve to fool the casual viewer.

For the viewer who is expecting the norm from Argento or for one who is not paying close attention, suspicion is cast upon Dr. Cavanna. Toward the end of the film, we experience Anna's terror as her doorbell rings repeatedly and there is a suspicious shadow on the building across the street. When the shadow is revealed to be Dr. Cavanna, we are far from relieved. His discussion with Anna also leaves little to enjoy. It seems apparent that Anna is the one who has killed Marie, and that Alfredo is truly dead (as the scene later alludes to before confirming), but Dr. Cavanna still seems suspicious to viewers. He knows too much. And Anna reveals too much. His demeanor becomes threatening, but that is simply because we are seeing it through Anna's eyes . . . as we have been seeing all the scenes for quite some time by this point. He is not the killer, though. As the astute viewer will have known it is Anna. Marco will soon learn thc samc.

That is the last red herring Argento will use in the film but is not the last bit of symbolism used by him. There is one more scene that gives an indication as to the fate of Anna Manni, and this is where Jesus fits into the film.

Anna, suffering a total mental breakdown and killing Marco, is chased by the police, who are sympathetic to her plight and are trying to help her. She does not see it this way, however, and we see their efforts through her eyes. Their looming faces and grasping hands are threatening and hostile from Anna's perspective. Eventually she falls onto the road and is picked up and carried to what one presumes is safety as the credits roll. If you find something familiar about the way she is carried it is because it matches how Jesus is held in Michelangelo's *Madonna della Pietà* statue.

The statue features Jesus in Mary's lap after the Crucifixion. Michelangelo thought it was important to not represent death with his statue, but instead to show the religious vision of abandonment. Argento uses this image of Anna to not only show that abandonment, but to also represent the impending resurrection of her soul. It is meant to convey that Anna has been broken as much as possible, but now she is on the path of healing, something that would have most likely been explored in the sequel he planned on filming but never did as of this writing.

It is easy to dismiss this film as a simple, ineffective *giallo* or rape revenge movie. It is just as easy to say it is a movie all about mental delusions.

When one looks at what Argento deliberately did with the film, its characters, symbols, and themes, one can only say that it is a movie that has far more depth than anything he has ever created up until that point in his career, and more depth than most (or maybe any) of the films that have come out of the *giallo* or rape revenge schools. It is a movie about the power of art and violence; the traumatic effects of rape and revenge, and the universal connection we have to these things; and, often overlooked, what the audience's role is when it comes to these types of films. Argento, whom many people wrongly consider to be a Freudian filmmaker, proves the power of Jungian archetypes of events and figures, which seems to suit his style of filmmaking more and really stands out here. In a word, the film is sublime.

And to think it almost turned out entirely different.

"AMERICA CAN SCREW ITSELF."

The Stendhal Syndrome as it exists today came close to being a very different film, which many Argento fans may have been happy with had it happened. The film has split Argento's supporters nearly down the middle, perhaps because it is unlike any film he has made before or since.

Argento has a long film history, which will be delved into later, but it was with his 1993 film, *Trauma*, that Argento tried his hand at making a movie in America. Prior to that, Argento filmed primarily in Italy and throughout Europe. He became considered a master filmmaker in Italy and gained a small but devoted following in America with die-hard horror fans. In America during the 1970s and 1980s if you were a fan of horror, but your local video rental store only carried films like *Halloween* (1978) and *A Nightmare on Elm Street* (1984), you were only getting part of the picture. Fans with access to a decent video store were exposed to foreign horror like *Pieces* (1982) and *Cannibal Holocaust* (1980). Among these foreign films, which were primarily Italian and Spanish, were the works of Dario Argento. His movies like *Suspiria* (1977), *The Bird with the Crystal Plumage* (1970), *Inferno* (1980), and *Opera* (1987), to name a small few, had earned him fans that were captivated by his sadistic and dream-like *gialli* and his unique horror films. His work was unlike anything coming out of

America, though it had influenced American films like *Halloween*, and hardcore horror fans loved it.

Despite that growing and vocal fanbase, Argento was not becoming a huge success in America. He had worked with American filmmakers before, most notably helping to secure financing for *Dawn of the Dead* (1978) and working with the director of that film, George Romero, for 1990's *Two Evil Eyes*. He had yet to fully do an American-shot film on his own and become as popular in America as he was in Italy. Enter *Trauma*, which caused much excitement among Argento fans when it was first announced. Here was the master working on American soil on a solo project. What could go wrong?

Nearly everything.

Argento wanted to be bigger in America. He already had the respect of many directors, but he also wanted to reach more fans. His bad experiences did not begin on *Trauma*, however. They really started with his collaboration with Romero on *Two Evil Eyes*. As Argento writes in his autobiography, *Fear* (Flesh and Blood Press, 2019), "When the film was released it was not the success we were looking for. George wasn't too pleased with his work during filming and in the sound editing phase we had some heated discussions. I criticized him for not being as committed as he should have been."

That was not enough to dissuade Argento from making a movie in America, but it offers Argento-like foreshadowing of what was to come. And while one would think it would sour him somewhat, it really endeared him to making a film in America.

Argento found himself surrounded by filmmaking peers and he loved it. He thought he had even found a new place to call home in Los Angeles. "At one point," he writes in *Fear*, "I said to myself that maybe I should never go back home." He loved the sense of film collaboration that everyone had in America, which was nearly the opposite of how it was in Italy where "directors don't ever meet each other, and when they do, they hardly talk."

He was laying down "roots" in America and shot his next film, *Trauma*, in Minneapolis. In his autobiography, however, he writes that when he returned to Rome on a break, he found it "impossible to leave" because it was so "beautiful."

Argento was being kind in his book. In fact, the only problem he really relates to *Trauma* is that the constant smoke effect they used on set damaged his health for years to come. There is also mention of the film not being well received. The facts of the matter are far more extreme and really soured the director's feelings on making films in America.

Alan Jones, a man who has written volumes on Dario Argento, quoted Argento as saying, "America can screw itself," in *Cinefantastique* (Vol. 27, no. 8) in 1996. That bold sentiment came from the director after being told by American casting directors that no American actresses would play the role of Anna in *The Stendhal Syndrome* as he had written the scenes. That feeling toward making films in America may have been less hostile if the making and reception of *Trauma* had been more positive.

Fans of Argento felt the director was making a mistake by shooting his film in America. In *Art of Darkness: The Cinema of Dario Argento – Director's Series 2*, edited by Chris Gallant (Flesh and Blood Press, 2000), there is an essay on *Trauma* written by Adrian Luther-Smith that sums up the situation quite nicely.

"Not unexpectedly, many of the director's [fans] sneered at their Italian idol for 'selling out.'" Luther-Smith goes on to write that it was understandable that Argento, who was tired of the poor distribution his films received outside of Italy, wanted to make films in America. His agent and other associates convinced him that making a movie in the US would "firmly establish his talent with a wider audience." Unfortunately, this would not be the case, as critics were not the kindest.

Jones, in *Profondo Argento* (Flesh and Blood Press, 2004), writes quite a bit about *Trauma* and reprints his write-up of the film for *Starburst* #178 (1993). The review, which is a fair review despite Jones' admitted great admiration of the director, ends with this bit of advice to the director. "Go back to Rome, Dario. Use your home location again in the way only you know how to milk its darkness and atmosphere. Forget all about the mass-market outside Italy. They don't care so you might as well give up trying to make them. Stop using American actors who can't cope with your baroque stylization." He goes on to write, "Bring back your galvanizing shocks to the system, your gore-soaked socks to the jaw of the genre. For *Trauma* is nothing more than a sloppy caress on the cheek."

The American actors did not help when it came to shooting that film, either. Piper Laurie and Frederic Forrest had their issues with the film and its director, despite a stated respect for the man. Jones, in that same piece in *Profondo Argento*, details these issues, the most disturbing of which is Laurie's take on the film.

Laurie first said that her advisors told her she would "be crazy not to work with Dario because of his fabulous reputation." She stated that she never knew where the camera was going while filming, but that it "greatly enhanced her performance" because of that. Before the film was released, she said she was "anxious" to see it. Later, however, she admitted to Jones at a film festival that she had not seen it.

"I found it impossible to see even on video," Laurie told the writer, "and I wasn't too bothered anyway because I'd heard I was terrible in it. I shouldn't be telling you this but both Frederic Forrest and I thought the whole film was a laugh. Neither of us thought the film made sense . . ." and they spent their time offscreen laughing at it together.

Working with the union, the film's producers, and distributor was not a pleasant experience for the director, either. Argento was used to working a certain way, which the union was at odds with, and the film's distributor and some of its producers wanted the excess gore and blood that Argento puts into his films to be toned down for American audiences.

Couple all of this with the fact that there were those naysaying the film before even seeing it because he cast his daughter, Asia, in it, and it seems like the film was doomed from the start. Argento was set to film *The Stendhal Syndrome* in America next, and his pick to play Anna Manni was Bridget Fonda, who, according to Dario Argento in *Fear*, broke off all contact once the director said he could see his daughter in the role of Anna. Jennifer Jason Leigh was also considered for the role. Before Dario Argento got too far into the beginning stages of the film, though, he decided he was done with America and all its problems and went back to Italy to shoot the film.

Had Argento stayed in America and shot with Fonda or Leigh, the film would have been so far removed from what he created it would probably not even resemble it in the slightest. Argento alluded to such in an interview published on April 17, 2019 with Christopher Bollen for *Interview*. Bollen asked Argento what draws him to *giallo*, and Argento's answer perfectly explains why *The Stendhal Syndrome* would not have worked if it had been set in America.

"*Giallo*," Argento explains, "is a potpourri of references. There was a torrent of themes and thoughts that agglomerated into Italian *giallo*. For example, let's not forget […] the unreal and highly artistic settings. Moreover, there's the Italian soul that marks the stories and characters – something coming from our past, our religion, and our superstitions."

I believe *The Stendhal Syndrome* also would have been a bigger disappointment than *Trauma* had it been filmed in America due to creative compromises Argento would have had to make. Instead, he created a film that divided his fans and critics and turned out to be a landmark film of sorts for Argento, Italy, *and* Italian filmmaking.

The Stendhal Syndrome marked a few notable firsts for Italian films. The movie was the first to be allowed to be filmed inside the Uffizi Gallery. That may not seem like a very important event for an American, but for a culture that values its art as much as Italy does, it was a huge moment in film and Italian history. Had Dario Argento not been the esteemed director that he was, it is unlikely he could have filmed there. Was it essential to the plot? No. Any museum with fine art in it could have sufficed for the opening. It did add to the film's authenticity, however, and its inclusion heralds back to the director's own experience with the very real Stendhal syndrome.

Argento has said he suffered from the Stendhal syndrome as a child while touring Athens with his parents. He was climbing the steps of the Parthenon and ended up in a trance-like state which caused him to become separated from his parents. He again thought of this traumatic experience when he came across Magherini's book on Stendhal syndrome and got the seed of an idea about the film he would eventually create.

As Argento admits in *Fear*, filming in Chicago or Phoenix (two places he looked for inspiration) would have totally changed the feel of the picture as there were no art museums that could compare to the atmosphere and fine art available in the Uffizi Gallery. Argento's film utilizes the overwhelming presence of art in so many of its scenes that it is hard to even picture what that would have played like had he decided to film in America. America is not an old enough country, and it does not have the appreciation for art that Italy possesses. In Argento's film, art is as much a character as is Anna Manni, and for Argento, who is an artistic filmmaker, filming in America would likely give the film more of an entertainment feel as opposed to an artistic one. Even the special effects that were utilized in the film have an artistic feel to them, though that has always been the case with Argento and his on-screen kills.

Argento, in part, rode to his height of fame based off his inventive and creative character kills. The violence he utilizes is in the standard excesses of Italian horror cinema of the 1970s and 1980s, which he really helped usher in, but his unique take on the violence treats it as an artform. This was not something American movies were doing at the time.

Whether it was the opening of *Suspiria*, with a hanging that involves the victim dropping through stained glass, or the needles under the eyes in *Opera*, Argento's stylized use of violence made audiences feel the pain while simultaneously celebrating it. This was, of course, not very different in *The Stendhal Syndrome*, where a razor is embedded in Alfredo's palm and then used to cut Anna's face in a caress, and where a bullet pierces a person's cheek in slow motion. In part, the kills are actually subdued in this film because Argento was working primarily on a psychological thriller. He also could have been more graphic with the rape scenes, but thankfully was not. The dampening of Argento's usual excess serves the film well, causing distress among viewers when that boundary is violated.

There is another area in *The Stendhal Syndrome*, however, where Argento forged new ground not only for himself, but also Italian filmmaking. That area, which seems ubiquitous to film now, is in the use of computer-generated imagery (CGI).

Argento had plenty of practical effects in *The Stendhal Syndrome*, and they worked exceedingly well. He also used CGI and was reportedly the first Italian director to do so in an Italian film. He had always wanted to use a shot of pills going down someone's throat from inside the body and had never been able to . . . until this film.

The use of CGI in the movie is primitive by today's standards. Even when the film came out, scenes like the pills going down the throat seemed a bit unrealistic. He also used the technique for scenes with the bullet going into the face, which works well, and for when the painting melts away and when Anna walks through one. Those scenes work far better than the pill scene, and at the time the film came out they looked amazing. They hold up now somewhat, too, but are not as seamless as today's CGI.

Argento's film is not an effects-heavy production, though, and it is not meant to be. He was aiming for something more cerebral with this film, and for many fans and critics, that was a turn off.

The film's initial reviews were unduly harsh, though that is somewhat understandable as most reviewers would have only seen the film once at that point. *Entertainment Weekly*, which uploaded the print review by Marc Bernardin to its site on August 13, 1999, called it a "snooze." Bernardin goes on to write, "*The Stendhal Syndrome* was made with a steady, practiced hand, but none of it is scary – except for the queasiness you'll feel knowing that the brutal rape scenes feature a young woman being directed by her daddy." The reviewer's feelings are made clear with the use of the word "daddy," but those are Bernardin's issues, not a fault of the film. It seems he was reviewing the movie based on what he understood Dario Argento's past films to be instead of actually viewing them.

Another mainstream publication to review the film was *Variety.* David Rooney wrote a piece on February 4, 1996, in which he seemed aware of Argento's past efforts. "Dario Argento," he writes, "tempers his penchant for Grand Guignolesque bloodletting and supernatural excess, returning to a style closer to that of his early thrillers."

Rooney's praise slowly evaporates, however, as he describes later parts of the film as "pure hokum," and says the second half of the film descends into "increasing silliness." He pointedly did not like Anna in the "bad Veronica Lake wig,' nor her transformation that came with that. Incidentally, it has been reported that Asia Argento also did not like that wig, and thought the film lost its way from that scene forward.

Time and multiple viewings seem to create a better understanding of the movie, as noted in the second edition of *Rape-Revenge Films: A Critical Study* by Alexandra Heller-Nicholas (McFarland Publishers, 2021). Heller-Nicholas obviously watched the film with an eye set to it being more than mere entertainment, though I would suggest it is also beyond a mere "rape-revenge" movie and does not fully embrace the tropes of that genre. Heller-Nicholas understands much of the symbolism Dario Argento utilizes throughout the movie, and states the movie is "about a woman literally trapped within the apparatus of artistic representation. In a meta-mirroring of the Stendhal syndrome condition itself, the film contrasts Anna's status as a fictional depiction of a rape survivor with the representational traditions that surround her both diegetically and extradiegetically – not only in regard to the Renaissance and Baroque rape imagery she sees in the Uffizi, but also in terms of the options film history has made available to her as either a tough tomboy or a vampish *femme fatale*."

Heller-Nicholas does a deep dive into the scene where Anna paints on herself, relating it to the historical patterns of rape and how the survivors are treated, all of it being fascinating and insightful reading. The author, however, acknowledges that the film is not "perfect," and that it is not the "kind of rape-revenge movie to which all should aspire," but does call it "valuable and unique."

In volume 156 of *Contemporary Film Directors* (University of Illinois Press, 2012) L. Andrew Cooper offers an interesting alternative look at the film. ". . . *The Stendhal Syndrome*," Cooper writes, "is about the misguided critics who condemn horror fictions for creating horrific realities. The film argues that only viewers as unstable as Anna run the risk of becoming killers in her footsteps."

While that is not a message normally brought up in discussions about the film, it does have merit. Cooper's further points reinforce the author's position.

"Argento's film attacks critical assumptions about the sadism and dangerousness of violent cinema, but it does not make cinema safe, and it does not provide easy answers to the questions it raises." That is agreeable, as is Cooper's assertion that interpretations in Argento's films are always "vexed." That is also the reason why Argento's films, and especially *The Stendhal Syndrome*, are so interesting. There is no one-size-fits-all explanation of what is being witnessed.

Troy Howarth, author of *So Deadly, So Perverse Vol. 1* (Midnight Marquee Press, 2015) and interviewed later in this book, provides an audio commentary for the Blu-ray disc of *The Stendhal Syndrome*. In it, he calls the film Argento's last great work at the time, claiming that after it, most of the director's films were lackluster and often more or less chasing trends. It is an accurate statement. Argento, during and after this film, started suffering from health and money problems. He blamed the smoke used on the set of *Trauma*, and he claims he was ripped-off by the people handling his money. Couple that with the negative criticisms of *The Stendhal Syndrome* and that he was again using his daughter in a perverse nepotism sort of way, and it all paints its own picture of what may have been happening in Argento's mind after the film was completed and seen by audiences. Howarth's argument that it was Argento's last great film leaves out the fact that it may have been his greatest film, period, and for a man with as rich a career as Argento's, that is saying something.

DARIO ARGENTO

DIRECTOR, WRITER, PRODUCER

The "Master of Horror" was born September 7, 1940, and it was thirty years later that his name became synonymous with the *giallo* for his directorial debut, *L'uccello dalle plume di cristallo* (1970), a film known in America as *The Bird with the Crystal Plumage*. That was not his first foray into movies, however.

Argento's first known work is an uncredited role as an actor (playing a priest) and writer in 1966's *Scusi, lei è favorevole o contrario?*, which translates into English as *Pardon, Are You For or Against?* From there he had 12 other projects (many of them Westerns) where he served as a writer before directing *The Bird with the Crystal Plumage*.

Argento's work as a writer, director, co-producer, and producer is well-known to any horror or Italian film fan. Some of the projects he has created or has been involved in creating, using the English titles, are *The Cat o' Nine Tails* (1971); *The Five Days* (1973); *Deep Red* (1975); *Suspiria*; *Dawn of the Dead* (1978), for which he edited a version of the film for European audiences; *Inferno* (1980); *Opera*; *Sleepless* (2001); *Mother of Tears* (2007); *Dracula 3D* (2012); and *Occhiali neri* (2022). There are so many more, however, including *Jenifer* (2005) for the *Masters of Horror* television series.

In Bollen's *Interview* piece that was referenced earlier, Argento clarified quite a few things about himself and his films. He talked about falling in love with horror at a young age and how the genre films were not "respected" by his "family or professors." "I felt bad for Hitchcock," Argento states, "and for those who, like me, felt part of this weird, alien clan." He goes on to discuss how Edgar Allan Poe served as a role model for him, not only for Argento's films, but for his own writing, which he did before making movies.

When he talks about his movies, one gets a very clear idea where films like *The Stendhal Syndrome* originated from. He says, "My films are always brought to life from an idea, a coincidence, or a dreamlike magic." And that is the key to understanding them. If looked at as a straight, standard narrative, they often become confusing or muddled, but looked at as "dreamlike magic," they make a perfect kind of sense.

Many books have been written about Argento, several of which I have cited previously. Some have delved into the psychology of his films. Others have examined the psychology of the director himself, where fascination with the fact that he often uses his own hands as the killer's hands in his films and casts his daughter in some controversial roles seem to rule the discourse. I will not go into all that, as the focus here is on a single film. I will state, however, that Argento may mean many things to different people, but *The Stendhal Syndrome* makes one aspect of the director obvious.

Argento is, above all else, a visionary filmmaker who wants his films to have a certain kind of perfection. His movies captivate despite the culture gap, but they also confuse just as easily. Yes, his work has slipped quality-wise in the years since *The Stendhal Syndrome* premiered, but is that from the exhaustion that sets in from trying to reach a goal when the odds are stacked against you in so many ways? I would suggest that the experience of making *Trauma* in America; the mixed reviews of *The Stendhal Syndrome*, which was a labor of love; and health and money issues all point to a man who is tired. He tried giving audiences what he wanted to give them, now he gives them what he thinks they want to see. Perhaps he is hoping more money will come in that will enable him to make the types of films he wants to make again someday.

Maybe not.

Regardless, Argento is, as of this writing, still directing and starring in movies. And his influence on directors continues to be felt worldwide from Quentin Tarantino to Gaspar Noé, who put Argento in a starring role in his 2021 film *Vortex*. Perhaps he never received the widespread respect he wanted from American cinema, but that influence has done more for cinema in general than any respect from Hollywood could have ever dreamed to accomplish. One would hope that influence would be carried on by his daughter, Asia, but her story is quite a bit different.

ASIA ARGENTO

ANNA MANNI

Asia Argento was born as Aria Maria Vittoria Rossa Argento September 20, 1975. She is the daughter of Dario Argento and Daria Nicolodi, an actress who often appeared in Dario Argento's films, such as *Opera*. "Asia" was not a name that could be put on the birth registry in Rome, so she was registered as Aria, but goes by Asia. She is a director, actress, writer, musician, and voice-over artist. She has also been the center of controversy in recent years with her inclusion in the #MeToo Movement, sexual assault allegations made against her by an at-the-time 17-year-old co-star in a film, and her implied (by some) role in the suicide of Anthony Bourdain. The sexual assault allegations and the implication of her role in the death of Bourdain seem to be the fallout of being the well-known and outspoken daughter of one of Italy's most famous directors, and she has been driven to shield herself from the media moreso than ever before in recent years. I used to have chats with her via social media, but once the allegations came out, those quickly stopped, and my multiple requests for an interview for this book went unanswered. That is all I will write about the controversies. Instead, I will focus on her career.

Argento's first role as an actress was in 1985 for the Italian TV mini-series *Sogni e bisogni*. A year later she was in *Demons 2*. From there forward it is a fairly steady career of acting, appearing and starring in such films as *The Church* (1989); *Queen Margot* (1994); *New Rose Hotel* (1998); *B. Monkey* (1998); *Scarlet Diva* (2000), which also was the first full-length feature she directed and wrote, and was the subject of my first weekly column for Filmthreat.com; *xXx* (2002); *The Heart is Deceitful Above All Things* (2004), which she also directed and wrote the screenplay for; *Land of the Dead* (2005); *Marie Antoinette* (2006); and the 2014 TV series *Mafiosa*.

In between acting in over 60 roles, she directed and wrote films such as the two mentioned previously. She also directed Marilyn Manson's video for "Saint" in 2004, the 2010 short film *42 One Dream Rush*, and *Misunderstood* (2014).

In an undated interview for Forcedexposure.com, Alan Bishop had an interesting discussion with the actress. The focus of the interview was on her music and cigarettes, but thoughts on her father and film came up during it as well.

". . . my father was a bit of a petite bourgeoise," Argento says, "I mean he knows everything about cinema, but my mother was the savant afficionado of music."

When the discussion turns to vinyl records and the death of that format, Argento likens it to the declared death of film, and this is where her thoughts on the medium come through loud and clear.

". . . to be quite honest, people predict the death of film," she says. "[T]he death of film, of 35 mm, of this beautiful medium, of the grain or lack of grain, something absolutely authentic, organic like film that is made out of trees, out of water, out of leaves, and to be replaced with something that duplicates reality like a robot, that's why my new movie, as a director, I insisted that it be shot on film." She did so because in "two years" they predicted that film would be "absolutely dead."

Argento goes on to explain that one of the reasons she loves making movies is because of their collaborative nature. She enjoys that about a lot of the art she does, including her music. Of course, Argento has her own thoughts on *The Stendhal Syndrome* as well.

In the featurette *Three Shades of Asia*, found on the Blue Underground Blu-ray release of the film, Argento reveals that the film has a very personal connection to her. Her character, Anna, was named after her sister, Anna Ceroli, who died in 1994. Argento also said that *The Stendhal Syndrome* was her favorite of the films she had done with her father up until that point.

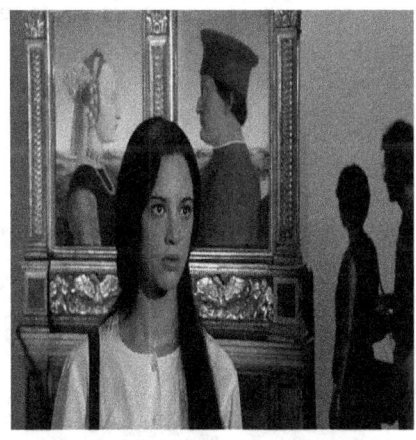

Not everything about the film was fondly remembered by her, however. Argento did talk about something that often comes up in discussion of the film, and that is the fact that her father filmed her in some horrific rape scenes.

Argento admits that some of the rape scenes left her "shaken," even though she had a body double. The scenes themselves are not as graphic as many of the scenes her father has filmed in other movies, but they are far more intimate and brutal despite lacking some of the director's normal excesses of cruelty.

Argento is well within her rights to judge those scenes that she was in, but what critics often seem to forget is that *The Stendhal Syndrome* is a film. Dario and Asia Argento are artists. They will do what they believe needs to be done for whatever project in which they are involved. To paraphrase what director Rob Zombie told actor Bill Moseley when Moseley noted that the gun rape scene in Zombie's *The Devil's Rejects* (2005) was starting to wear on the cast and crew: art isn't safe. And it should not be. Sometimes it is necessary to be pushed past one's limits so that great art can be created. That is something Asia Argento understands very well, but many critics seem to have a hard time comprehending.

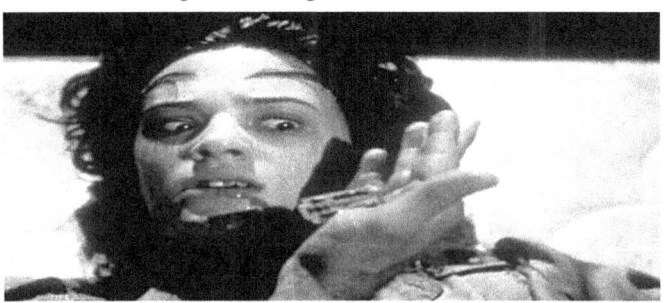

THOMAS KRETSCHMANN

ALFREDO

Kretschmann was born September 8, 1962 in East Germany, where he would flee from later in his twenties. According to an interview he gave to *The Korea Times*, which was published July 27, 2017, growing up and later fleeing East Germany helped form his "view of the world." "I arrived in Yugoslavia first, which adopted neither capitalism nor communism. The country remembers massacres taking place when it was being split up." It is a good thing he fled his birth country, or the world may never have gotten to see him perform in some of the biggest films to appear on screen.

With over 130 acting credits in television and screen to his name, Kretschmann got his start in 1985 in the role of a soldier for *Westler - East of the Wall*. Two years later he got a role on the television series *Hals über Kopf*, and the ball started rolling from there. Some of the other television shows and movies he has appeared in include *Stalingrad* (1993); *Queen Margot* (1994), where he met Asia Argento; *Nachtbus* (1995); *Prince Valiant* (1997); the television series *Total Recall 2070* (1999); the fondly remembered *Relic Hunter* (1999-2000) television series; *U-571* (2000); *Blade II* (2002); *The Pianist* (2002); the television series *24* (2003); *King Kong* (2005); *Valkyrie* (2008); *Cars 2* (2011); *Dracula 3D*; *Captain America: The*

Winter Soldier (2014); *Avengers: Age of Ultron* (2015), where he reprised his role of Baron von Strucker from *Captain America: The Winter Soldier*; *Dragged Across Concrete* (2018); the incredible *Infinity Pool* (2023); and *Indiana Jones and the Dial of Destiny* (2023).

It is quite a wide range of roles from a man who never seems to slow down.

Dario Argento, who, as noted previously, directed Kretschmann in *Dracula 3D*, revealed why he worked with the actor again on the movie during an interview with Peter Sobczynski for RogerEbert.com, which was published October 24, 2013.

"With Kretschmann," Argento says, "he has a real European face that is right for Dracula. We worked together before and when I asked him, he said that it was his dream to play Dracula." While giving Kretschmann credit for having a "European face," it should also be noted that the man can act, which is why he has been given so many roles in so many prominent features. His dedication to his roles was no different in *The Stendhal Syndrome*, as noted by James Gracey in his biography, *Dario Argento* (Oldcastle Books, 2010).

Gracey writes that Kretschmann "plays Alfredo as a deranged monster with no redeeming qualities." When rehearsing, Kretschmann "practised [sic] rolling a real razor blade around in his mouth for the infamous scene where Alfredo produces a razor from his mouth and slashes Anna's face with it." He also writes that "Kretschmann improvised quite a lot and Argento was accommodating of this; a notable improvisation appears when Alfredo simulates oral sex with a gun."

Kretschmann may have been playing a "deranged monster," but his acting skills *and* good looks took the role of Alfredo to another dimension, perhaps making him one of the most evil and memorable antagonists in Argento's filmography.

TROY HOWARTH

AUTHOR

Howarth, as mentioned previously, did a commentary track on the release of *The Stendhal Syndrome* that I watched for this book. As I was writing the first draft and reaching out for interviews, I contacted him because I found his insights on the commentary track to be invaluable when it came to this film.

Howarth attributes his love of film, especially horror films, to his mother, who passed away in 2015. "She was a big fan of horror films," he says, "especially Hammer and so on. To give some perspective, my maternal grandmother was aware of my love of horror – and she died shy of my third birthday! She told my mom that I was nuts about this stuff because she was watching things like *The Omen* [1976] and *Rosemary's Baby* [1968] when she was pregnant with me." That love of horror runs so deep that he "literally" cannot remember a time he was not into it.

Howarth's passion for horror eventually led him to the films coming out of Italy, starting with Mario Bava's *Baron Blood* (1972). Howarth explains, "It was on the late movie, and my mom recorded it. When I watched it, I couldn't articulate what it was, but I knew there was something different about it. It just had a weird sort of flavor, though I was far too young to understand anything about it being a foreign film or who Bava was or any of that." His experience watching the film mirrors a lot of fans' encounters with foreign horror films at an early age. It was not until he was a little "older," which, according to him, means he was around eight or nine years of age, that he finally started to get an idea of what he had witnessed.

"I begged my parents to buy me a copy of *The Encyclopedia of Horror Movies* [HarperCollins, 1987] edited by Phil Hardy," Howarth states. "It was the softcover edition with Jack Nicholson's face peering through the door in *The Shining* [1980] on the cover. It was way above my intellect for that age – I was just fascinated by all the pictures and write-ups of movies I had never heard of. They covered all these films with foreign titles and that confused me at that age." It was within this book where he found the film he had seen and not forgotten years earlier.

"I saw a picture of Elke Sommer in *Baron Blood*," Howarth explains, "which they identified as *Gli orrori del castello di Norimberga* – the Italian title. It was there that I started to recognize that the film's director, Mario Bava, was a major director in horror films and that *Baron Blood* supposedly wasn't even one of his better films. So that intrigued me!"

Baron Blood may have been Howarth's first unintentional foray into the realm of foreign horror, but it was far from his last. Over time, he started to take in more and more Italian and Euro horror that he saw on either late-night television or on VHS. He saw films such as *Beyond the Door* (1974), *The Night Evelyn*

Came Out of the Grave (1971), *Zombie* (1979), and more.

"But at that time," Howarth explains, "I was put off by the dubbing and the somewhat, let's say, loose plotting. So, it took me a while to really develop that passion for Italian horror."

Howarth graduated high school and with his parents' permission, took a year off before starting college. As a condition of taking that break, he had to continue working. He had already started working at McDonald's in high school and kept that job. Howarth states, "My friends had all splintered off to various areas away [from me], and I didn't really have a lot to do with my money, so I started buying more and more VHS bootlegs through Midnight Video – they were a big grey market dealer at that time." It was a path many horror fans went down during that era, as it was pre-Internet and places like Vinegar Syndrome and Severin Films, which have a passion for putting out obscure movies, had yet to exist, and now Howarth had a mission.

"I had developed a yen to get a better version of *Baron Blood* – my copy was the one mom had recorded and it had seen better days – but was disappointed when I saw the HBO pre-record was now out of print and not available. Shortly after, I was looking in *Fangoria* and sure enough, Elite Entertainment was issuing *Baron Blood* and *Lisa and the Devil* [1973] as a double-feature laser disc . . . and not just that, but these would be the uncut European versions to boot! From there, I got the itch, and I started picking up all

101

the Bava films I had missed that Midnight Video had to offer." Howarth broadened his horizons and started obtaining films by Argento, Lucio Fulci, and Jess Franco. "Nearly 30 years later," he says, "and I'm still obsessed."

Howarth's love for movies eventually turned into a writing career that revolved around them. He explains, "I started off writing what I thought would be a magazine article on Mario Bava, then it grew and became a book – *The Haunted World of Mario Bava* [Flesh and Blood Press, 2002]. It was the first book in English on Bava and was first published in 2002. I then had a crisis of confidence – not unusual for me – and that led to a long period of writing reviews online but not doing any more books. I finally got back into the swing of things by doing a revised version of the Bava book for an American publisher once the rights with the UK publisher [. . .] lapsed in 2012. From there, I've written about 15 books covering everything from *giallo* cinema to Spanish horror icon Paul Naschy and American genre legend John Carpenter."

Books were not the only thing he was doing related to movies, either. He also started diving into something he originally developed an interest in with the laser discs: movie commentaries.

"Like so many," Howarth states, "I started listening to [commentaries] in laser disc days, and I suppose I always had some hope of getting a chance to do one once I became a fan of the form – but I never really thought it would happen. I always loved listening to Carpenter and Werner Herzog and George

Romero and David Cronenberg among filmmakers; among critics and historians." Howarth liked what people like Sir Christopher Frayling, Jonathan Rigby, David Kalat, and Gregory Mank did with their own commentaries. He also learned what he did not like in a commentary by listening to those that either bored or irritated him.

Howarth eventually found himself getting into the commentary game. "When Michael Mackenzie at Arrow Video gave me a chance to do one for *The Night Evelyn Came Out of the Grave*, I leapt at it – I was a bundle of nerves and figured it would be a one-and-done thing, but it went over well and as of now I've done about 130-some tracks, either solo or with co-commentators. I've done plenty of films by Argento, Fulci, Umberto Lenzi, etc., – and a wide array of films in other genres, too, including two by Polanski (*Bitter Moon* [1992] and *The Tenant* [1976]) and even an early Hitchcock called *Rich and Strange* [1931]. My interests are rich and varied, so I always enjoy the challenge of trying something unexpected."

As previously noted, Howarth's commentary on *The Stendhal Syndrome* is what prompted me to contact him for an interview. In addition to being a highly informative and interesting commentary, Howarth really understood the film. One thing he said really stood out to me. It was his statement that, at the time the commentary was recorded, *The Stendhal Syndrome* was Argento's last great film. I had to ask him more about that, and his answer to that and to whether it was still true is just as interesting as the commentary he did for the film.

"Fandom is a fickle and funny place," Howarth begins. "Fans love their idols until they stumble, then they seem to get a perverse pleasure out of saying how they've 'lost it' and should just 'hang it up.' That's such an arrogant and insufferable position, so I will answer by stressing that Argento doesn't owe us fans anything. We are in his debt for all the great films he made. Sometimes artists evolve and change, and we don't like that change. Sometimes they become obsessed with new things, and we find ourselves missing the good old days. And sometimes talent can atrophy with time for various reasons. But look at William Friedkin, for example. He had a run of not-very-inspired work that ran for years, then he came out of nowhere with *Bug* [2006] and showed that he still 'had it.'"

Howarth continues. "My own feeling has been that even if Argento never makes another good film, he's still given me so many that I love and hold dear that it doesn't much matter. Obviously, I'd love to see him make some more good films, but he doesn't owe it to me or anybody else. And if he's happy doing what he's doing, then I want him to continue making movies for as long as he wants. It's not my place or anybody else's to say he should 'think of his legacy' and retire."

With that sentiment on an artist's responsibility out of the way, Howarth goes on to explain Argento's legacy and why *The Stendhal Syndrome* may be his last great picture at the time of this interview.

"Argento's really great run of box office successes ended in the mid-80s with *Phenomena* [1985] and *Demons* [1985]," Howarth continues. "The stuff after that tended to suffer from spottier distribution for a whole slew of reasons, and gradually his production empire collapsed amid financial difficulties. *Opera* did very well in Italy and various other foreign markets, but the proposed release in the US through Orion fell through when Orion ended up in financial problems, and it just didn't get the wide exposure it truly deserved; it was also a very lavish and expensive film, so that it didn't get that kind of release was a bad omen of things to come."

That was not the end of Argento's troubles, either. Howarth explains, "He elected to go to America in 1989 to make an anthology film based on the writings of his idol, Edgar Allan Poe – originally it was to be four stories, each directed by a major genre name: Argento, Romero, Carpenter, and Stephen King, specifically. That fell through and it ended up being two directors, Dario and Romero, and the catchy title was *Two Evil Eyes*. It was designed to be Argento's breakthrough into the US market, which was never destined for success for various reasons. Argento achieved a rarefied level of success and stardom in Italy as a genre filmmaker – that's not something that happens so much in the US, where horror is traditionally ghettoized. Added to which, Argento's films tend to be a bit weird . . . not something the mainstream Cineplex audience in the US was going to embrace. *Suspiria* had been a big hit, but that was a one-off; typically, his stuff really didn't strike a huge chord with audiences in the US. And critics don't tend to take his stuff seriously."

All of this added up to a bad experience for the film and the director. "*Two Evil Eyes* got hardly any play in the US, and it did badly in Italy. Very badly." Howarth continues. "Then he decided to try again with *Trauma*, and it was another flop. His business was floundering in Italy and his attempt to penetrate the US market had failed. He was, in short, in deep shit."

As I wrote earlier, this all may have worked out for the best as the director returned to Italy. Howarth agrees. "Going back to Italy made sense," he says, "though *Stendhal* was originally conceived as an American film to be shot in Arizona, with maybe Bridget Fonda in the lead. Argento then retooled it as his Italian comeback film. It was eagerly anticipated, and he was still able to command the kind of money and, crucially, time that he needed to do his best work. It was, for all intents and purposes, an A-level production."

Howarth goes deeper into his explanation. "I think it also allowed him to exorcize his frustration with the censorship and production limitations imposed on him in the US and to also channel the darkness and depression he had felt over the death of his stepdaughter. The end result was his darkest and most introspective film. It's bleak and it's despairing. He had made very violent films before, notably *Opera*, but this was a different kind of violence. First of all, sexual violence had never been a feature in his films, though he flirts with it in *The Bird with the Crystal Plumage* and *Tenebre* [1982]. Second, this is a film that opens where a lot of his other films end – it examines the psychological scars of violence and what it can do to people. His protagonists seldom escape unscathed in his earlier films, and often there was a sense of a psychological break from reality by the protagonists at the end of the picture, but then the movie is over, and we fade to black. Here we stay with a woman who has been repeatedly brutalized as she tries to cope with what has happened and to get back to some sense of normality."

Howarth continues, "It's a very bleak, despairing movie and it hits me far harder, emotionally, than any of his other films. It's also beautifully realized by a top-notch crew of collaborators, like Fellini's former cameraman Giuseppe Rotunno. It shows an artist in control given the tools he needs to make a great film – and that was something that would come to an end after *Phantom of the Opera* [1998], which I'm one of the few people in the world who actually truly likes that film. But commercially, it was a fiasco, and the films which followed haven't made much of a dent either, so the budgets have shrunk along with the schedules, making it difficult for him to really deliver like he did when he was still on top.

"All of which is a long-winded way of saying, yes, I think it's his last great film to date. I'm hopeful *Occhiali neri* will be a welcome return to form, but his last three films have been very poor, in my opinion. Still, I think there's always room for hope that, so long as he's making films, he may deliver another worthy one. I'm not one for writing off favorite artists."

I asked Howarth how he feels *The Stendhal Syndrome* compares not only to Argento's own body of work, but also to other films of its kind. His answer, once again, is as direct as it is astute.

"It's a very unorthodox *giallo*," he states, "which is perhaps part of the reason it continues to divide fans. It's not really a conventional mystery at all, at least not in the long run. Like I said, it's his bleakest, most disturbing film by far. It's not 'fun' in the way that his other films tend to be. I love it for being so uniquely its own thing and for sticking to its guns in delving into such unpleasant subject matter. He avoids any kind of bad taste eroticism in the treatment of rape, and he makes it appropriately ugly and unpleasant – too much so for some, though I think it's entirely appropriate. It's almost as if getting this dark was disconcerting to him, as much of his work feels a lot more tongue-in-cheek. Maybe it was partly the way it was received, or maybe it was partly he didn't want to delve any deeper into that black abyss. It's hard to say."

That all leads to what would have happened had the film been shot in America with a different actress in the role of Anna. How did Howarth think the film would have turned out?

"I think it would have been very different," Howarth answers. "As I mentioned earlier, Bridget Fonda was supposed to play the lead; she had also been earmarked for a role in *Trauma*, but that fell through. Probably down to budget, though maybe it was scheduling since Fonda is reportedly a big fan. Anyway, that didn't pan out and there was some talk of getting Jennifer Jason Leigh. These are fine actresses who would have helped get the film some exposure, but I just don't see it being the same film or a happy experience in general. He wouldn't have had the same freedom, and I suspect he would have met resistance when it came to the more extreme or bizarre content. It would have been curious to have seen what would have happened with his career had he stayed in the US, but the whole idea of achieving the level of fame and success he had achieved in Europe was destined to remain a pipedream, I suspect."

Of course, Asia Argento, much to the ire of some, landed the role of Anna. I asked what Howarth thought of her performance and the many changes the character went through throughout the film.

"Asia is a very interesting personality," Howarth says. "She's always had this 'I don't give a fuck what you think' relationship with the Italian press, which made her a pariah long before her involvement with #MeToo – and the subsequent disgrace of being accused of sexually abusing an underage actor."

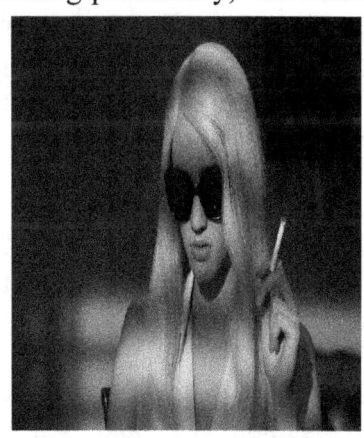

Howarth continues, "As an actress, she is capable of great things – but after a certain point it became clear that she really didn't have her heart in it anymore. She wanted to direct her own films, which she's done with some success. This is undoubtedly her finest work as an actor and it's one of the finest performances to feature in any of Argento's films – for me, it's up there with David Hemmings in *Deep Red* and Max von Sydow in *Sleepless*. It's a tough part, but she does it beautifully. If there's a nit to be picked, it's her age. She was just 20 when she made it, which makes the idea of being an inspector a little tough to swallow. But she's so good, honestly, I don't really care. She nails it. She goes to some very dark places and the fact that Dario has always been comfortable putting her into roles that require her to be victimized or to show her body raises a lot of eyebrows."

That fact comes up in nearly every professional review of the film . . . by writers who are not always well-versed in Dario Argento's filmography. Many a critic is quick to read something sinister or impure into this, but Howarth has what I think is the most accurate take on it.

"I think it's partly cultural – we're much more puritanical in the US – and it's also as he said: on set, she's an actress like any other, and he wouldn't ask her to do anything he wouldn't ask another performer in the same role," he says. "The way she changes from assertive to submissive back to assertive is quite remarkable. She handles all those shifts beautifully."

Howarth does express some disappointment with one aspect of how Asia Argento was in the film, though it is not the actor's fault.

"The sad part is when they did the English track," Howarth explains. "Dario bowed to pressure to get a girl with a softer voice to do the lines in English. This was absurd as it was shot in English (there's some production sound used in the film, for sure), and Asia is very comfortable with the language. But he caved on the point, and she was very pissed about it – and rightly so. This makes the English dub automatically worthless to me; it works much better in Italian, where her voice is present. Still, if they could ever rescue the production audio and create a new English dub, I'd be very interested to hear it."

I mentioned to Howarth that I found *The Stendhal Syndrome* to be much like *Angel Heart* (1987), in that it really rewards viewers who watch it multiple times. I asked Howarth if he agreed with that assertion.

"I think that is true of most Argento films," Howarth responds, "and really of most films by interesting filmmakers in general. Some people will never revisit films, and I don't understand that at all. I love going back and picking up on little nuances and starting to dissect. I'm not capable of doing that based on one viewing – it takes several, I find, to really come to grips with it. That's definitely true of *The Stendhal Syndrome*."

As the interview wound down, I wanted to delve more deeply into the viewers' reactions to the film. I think the film works differently for first-time Argento viewers than it does for those familiar with his work. I was wondering if Howarth felt the same way. His thoughts on the subject went to a place I, quite frankly, had not really ventured into.

Howarth explains, "I'm often asked what the ideal Argento 'primer' is, and I tend to think that [*The Bird with the Crystal Plumage*] remains a very good starting point." He thinks this because it is Argento's first film and because it has "an engaging quality that eases you into [Argento's] thematic obsessions without it being quite as challenging as some of the later ones." When it comes to *The Stendhal Syndrome*, though, Howarth says, "It would indeed be interesting to see how somebody who has never seen an Argento film would react to this; I've never had the pleasure, personally. It's a very difficult film, though also very obviously an outgrowth of what he had been doing for years. In fact, Michael Mackenzie wrote a very insightful essay for my book *Murder by Design: The Unsane Cinema of Dario Argento* [Midnight Marquee Press, 2020] which argues that *Stendhal* could be seen as a prequel of sorts to *Bird*, which is very interesting. Personally, I always saw it as a bit of an update of Bava's Gothic horror *The Whip and the Body* [1963] in which the sado-masochistic relationship between Daliah Lavi and Christopher Lee extends beyond the grave. Argento has never specifically mentioned *Whip*, but he would have seen it back in his early days as a reviewer for *Paese Sera*, so who knows . . . maybe some aspects of it lodged in his brain. Or it could just be a good old-fashioned coincidence. We critics and fans sometimes see homages where there are simply coincidences."

But what about the audience reaction to the film? What does Howarth think about how it divided fans upon its release, and does he agree with me that as time has passed people have started to accept the film more than when it was originally released? His answer surprised me, as it really exemplified the issues *The Stendhal Syndrome* caused for fans.

"At the time," Howarth begins, "it was eagerly anticipated as Argento's grand return to Italy following the commercial disappointment of his time in America. It was covered with great enthusiasm by the Italian press and there was a great deal of excitement. It opened strong – then it gradually died down. It was still a commercial success, certainly moreso than *Two Evil Eyes* or *Trauma* had been, but it wasn't as big as it had been hoped. By comparison, much of his work from the '70s and '80s had been much more popular at the box office. I'm sure a lot of this was down to it not being the film people expected. I know when I saw the film for the first time, I was a bit perplexed. Not disappointed, really, but it wasn't what I was expecting at all."

That sentiment seemed to echo what a lot of people were saying of the film. It was not what was expected, and there was a reason for this, as Howarth goes on to explain.

"When Argento talked about wanting to make his most violent film, fans expected something more like *Opera* or *Tenebre*. This was something else altogether,

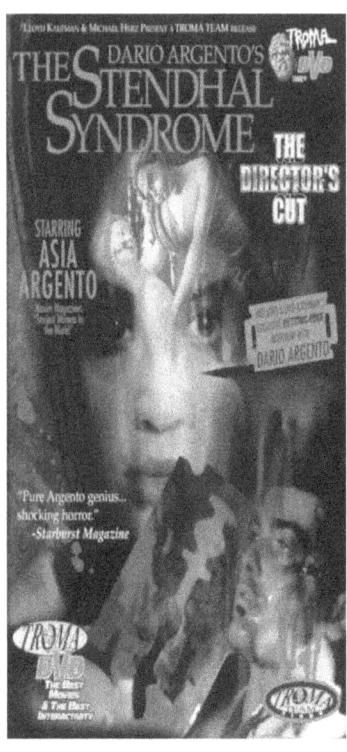

and it threw people. I think also, the fact that it wasn't a conventional *giallo* also disappointed many viewers. People complained it was predictable, when it really wasn't going for that sort of guessing game aspect that his earlier films had done."

Howarth continues, "It didn't help, too, that when it first arrived in the US – first via a dupe of the Japanese laser disc, then through the Troma label – it did so in a very ugly transfer. That Troma handled it at all is still one of the biggest puzzlers of Dario's career. He's not a bad businessman at all, but somehow he was tricked into thinking that Troma was going to give it a proper release and of course, they didn't – it barely played in theatres, which obviously pissed him off to no end. It wasn't until Blue Underground went back and did the special edition release for the Blu-ray that it finally got the release it deserved, which really allowed fans to enjoy it and appreciate it as intended."

Howarth concludes his thoughts on the matter by saying, "I suppose it will always be divisive since, again, it's not a 'fun' film. It's dark and it's disturbing. It deliberately leaves a sour aftertaste. I don't mind that, personally, but for some fans it's just too much and they tend to reject it. I do think the film's stock has risen dramatically over time and more people seem to be appreciating it now, which is wonderful. Again, while I like a number of the films Argento made after it, I think this was the last one that really came together in a wholly organic way and that really packs a true emotional wallop. It's great filmmaking [and] a great filmmaker still in full command of the medium."

As the interview ends, I ask Howarth if he has anything to add. Ever the gentleman, Howarth says, "[Nothing] except to say thank you for involving me in this project. And to thank you, too, for helping to bang the drum in favor of the film. As I mentioned [before], its reputation has improved over time – whereas films like *Trauma* and *Phantom* seem to have remained undervalued more-or-less consistently – but it still deserves further serious attention. I think it's one of the best films Argento ever made – and that, in itself, is a major achievement."

I could not agree more.

"WORKS OF ART HAVE POWER OVER US. GREAT WORKS OF ART HAVE GREAT POWER."

This chapter's heading quote is from the dubbed version of the movie, and it exemplifies how I feel about *The Stendhal Syndrome*. It is a powerful, great work of art that has so many different meanings to viewers. To some, it is a straight-ahead *giallo*, though one that may not be as potent, traditional, or as mysterious as Dario Argento's previous endeavors. To others it is an examination of what happens to an assault survivor and the destructive path of revenge. Some see it as Argento's take on the critics who say his films lead audiences to commit acts of violence and to show that by watching it you are just as guilty as he is for making it. And to some it is just a great story filled with foreshadowing and symbolism done in a way that is purely Argento.

Of course, there is a very vocal group that does not appreciate it as much as it does Argento's earlier works. The group states it is not a "real" *giallo*, the story is too hallucinatory, and that Argento filming his daughter in such situations detracts from the overall movie. Perhaps these are all valid claims, but none of them destroy the uniqueness of this film or the masterful storytelling that is orchestrated on screen.

There is also a large group of viewers that says the film takes on such a shift in tone part of the way through that it ruins the entire movie. What these viewers do not seem to realize is that this is not a tonal shift, but a narrative shift, and that it is as deliberate as the first half of the film. It, like every single shot in the movie, is constructed to take you to a certain place mentally. This narrative shift makes you watch the story unfold through Anna's eyes. It is jarring when one first views the film, but if you pay careful attention, you realize what is happening . . . and it is nothing short of brilliant filmmaking.

All these criticisms of the film do nothing to hamper Argento's underrated masterpiece. These criticisms are much like Anna's character after her bout of Stendhal syndrome at the beginning of the film: unaware of anything but their immediate surroundings and confused by them. They experience the film as a series of scenes, rather than a story that unfolds, not in a way they are familiar with, but as seen through the eyes of a traumatized character. It is a film that could have only been made by Dario Argento, in Italy, using the actors he did.

In *Fear,* Argento writes, "I've always been a lucky man because I've always been able to say what I wanted." This freedom gave him the strength and ability to tackle his own childhood traumatic experience with Stendhal syndrome.

Argento went to Greece with his parents when he was about fourteen years of age. He recounts in *Fear* that they visited the Parthenon. "I was hypnotized in front of that work of art." His book describes how he started to hear and see things. He states he felt like he was "sucked in" and then when he regained his senses his parents were nowhere to be found.

This incident planted the seed that many decades later would grow into what is Argento's most powerful film. He also admits in his biography that some of his fandom does not agree with my sentiment. In fact, that fandom often says his latest film, whichever it is, is his worst one, but he does not worry. "I do not take it too badly," he writes. "Tastes change, all one has to do is wait."

I believe *The Stendhal Syndrome* will eventually be considered one of his best if not the very best of his films by most critics and film historians. Argento may have always been more afraid of the bedroom corridor than the dark, as he writes in *Fear*, but in *The Stendhal Syndrome* he taps into far bigger and universal fears. He taps into the ones that really matter.

The Stendhal Syndrome is filled with fears that are far from the supernatural of some of Argento's other beloved films. And they go far deeper than those produced by the black-gloved hands in many of his *giallo* works. In this film he tackles loss. Loss of identity. Loss of free will. Loss of control. These are fears that are universal and terrifying. Argento's film shows that the outcome of these things is not always pleasant, and the act of revenge is not always the end of the pain. It is a message you will not get from films like *Opera* or *Deep Red*. Perhaps that is another reason his fans are so divided on this film. There are those who never want a director to grow or to venture into unfamiliar territory. Argento not only did both here, but he teased his longtime viewers throughout the film, toying with their expectations and refusing to give them what they were expecting.

Argento's obvious red herrings on the identity of the killer after Alfredo had supposedly been killed were just a minor part of that teasing. Using the Stendhal syndrome itself to lend an air of hallucination to the proceedings gave the film a surreal feel, so much so that some viewers may have believed Anna when she said the killer was still inside her controlling her thoughts. These things were so blatantly false that I cannot help but think Argento was manipulating an expectant audience, setting them up for something that would not have made sense, but that they were waiting for anyway. And had the film been made in America without Asia Argento, who is not to say that is the way the film would have gone? Dario Argento needed to get out of America and its alien way of filmmaking so he could recharge and reconnect with what he loved about the medium. He needed the home field advantage, and when he got it, he won the game.

Ultimately, it is how the general audience and critics see a film that determines its place in cinematic history. While there is no consensus on the merit of *The Stendhal Syndrome*, it seems clear that history will *not* rank it up there with some of the director's other works like *Suspiria* or *The Bird with the Crystal Plumage*, though it should. Fans and critics all tend to agree that those two films are hallmarks of Argento's work and cinema itself. While *The Stendhal Syndrome* is a more polished and mature work than those two pictures, it is also a film that lends itself to misunderstanding and irreconcilable expectations. From fans who wanted more of the same to critics who thought the director peaked several films ago, *The Stendhal Syndrome* suffered from those expectations. It may not have suffered as much had *Trauma* not been considered such a weak film, but then if that were the case, it may have meant that Argento's American filmmaking experience would have gone more smoothly and he would have made *The Stendhal Syndrome* in America as well, lessening the movie's impact all around. We shall, thankfully, never know.

Argento may have, for a time, lamented the fact that he never became as big as Hitchcock in America. He may have been upset that his biggest fame "only" came from Italy. But he knows he is respected around the world not only by film fans, but by directors as well. In *Fear* he writes of going to conventions throughout the world and being received with accolades, often by audiences that get younger and younger. He knows he is accepted. He knows he is respected. Is it enough?

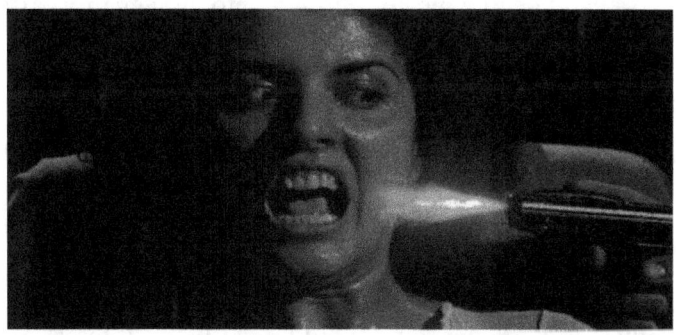

Only the director can answer that, but there is cause for consideration. *The Stendhal Syndrome* is a very personal film. Argento puts a bit of himself in all his films in one way or another, but this film is different. He suffered from a bout of the syndrome as a child, and it resonated with him. He cast his daughter in the title role, in a move that had people shaking their heads in disbelief and disgust. It also, in a few ways, does seem to be a response to critics who say his work affects people in a negative way. At its core, it is Argento's statement on the power of art, be it paintings, sculpture, or film. Looking at the film from the eyes of an artist reveals layers one initially mistook as something else entirely. Taken together, it serves to make this the most personal of his films . . . and one that could truly only come from his mind. He put to film what he intended to be seen. What audiences brought to it was of their own making, and because of that the film remains to be mistaken for something else entirely.

Howarth says the film could be Argento's last great work, and he may be correct. Argento, however, is still a master even when he has lost his way. His unique, nightmarish vision lends such a unique and personal touch to his films that it is hard to imagine them in anyone else's hands. This is especially true of *The Stendhal Syndrome.* Some of his fans may not adore it, and some film journalists may miss the point, but the blueprint of the film is as clear as day. None of those critics could name anyone who could do it better, either, or someone who would even be an interesting substitute for the director. Not even directors he has inspired like Tarantino, John Carpenter, and James Wan could have made this film in such an effective way.

As a fan of *The Stendhal Syndrome* and the director, it is rather disheartening to see the reactions to the film, the director, and his later works. If one was to be perfectly honest, however, there is some merit behind that sentiment.

The Stendhal Syndrome works best when you immerse yourself into it, much like Anna was drawn into the classic works of art. It rewards viewers who have a knowledge of art, Argento's past films, *giallo*, and the psychological impact of horrendous crimes. It demands attention, and if one cannot or will not devote all the attention it needs, it *does* come off as a disjointed narrative that may be confusing in many ways.

As for Argento, he may have been (and by many is still considered to be) a master of Italian cinema. His contributions to film are not disputed by anyone. His lack of "success" in America, however, has troubled him, but it was also inevitable. Quite simply, Argento does not make American movies. He does not even really make Italian films. He makes Argento films. Movies that are keenly attuned to his vision. His cultural nuances may be easier to follow or ignore than that of his Japanese counterparts, but his unique way of storytelling alienates American viewers because far too many of them are used to having their plots spoon fed to them. He may be a name in American horror culture, but he was never meant to be a household name in America the same way he is in Italy, and it has nothing to do with his lack of filmmaking skills and everything to do with his signature filmmaking. Unfortunately, his filmmaking has lapsed.

There is no argument that the quality of Argento's films has decreased over the last few years. *Dracula 3D* is often pointed out as exemplifying the problem. Critics say it is Argento responding to trends and gimmicks in film. While the film is regrettably forgettable, it is no surprise that the master of horror would do a vampire film. It's also no surprise that a director who embraced CGI before any other Italian director would utilize 3D. But that film and a few others after *The Stendhal Syndrome* do come across as uninspired.

Argento has lived a full life. Having his money stolen, having health problems, not gaining the success in America that he sought – all these things have had an impact on him. Audiences also change.

It is hard to admit that a director I admire has perhaps lost his way, or that he is no longer as good at his craft as he used to be. I will continue watching his films, however, as long as he puts them out. I will watch each one hoping it shows a return to greatness. If he never recaptures that spark, I will still have *The Stendhal Syndrome*, and I can't see anyone, not even Argento, doing anything that even comes close to what he achieved with it.

###

Index

Doug Brunell is the author of the critically-acclaimed novels *Nothing Men* and *Black Devil Spine*. His interests include film, rare books, and monitoring earthquakes for occult activity. He currently resides in Northern California. #HumboldtHorror

Other Works by Doug Brunell

Novels

NOTHING MEN - For years there have been rumors of inhuman things inhabiting the forests and mountains that make up the Trinity Alps of Northern California. Bigfoot. UFOs. Ghosts. Vampires. One family is about to learn the truth about these rumors as their summer vacation quickly turns into a one-way trip to Hell. No one is safe and nothing is sacred when dealing with the Nothing Men. Available in paperback and for eReaders.

"Nothing Men made me think about the likes of Herschell Gordon Lewis, Tobe Hooper, and prompted flashbacks of films like *The Wicker Man* and [the] *Texas Chainsaw Massacre*." --cinema-crazed.com

BLACK DEVIL SPINE - Dan Gere is a bestselling author in desperate need of another book idea. When he meets Martin Springer, a reclusive painter and fetish photographer, it seems he has discovered the solution to his problem. What follows, however, is a sickening descent into insanity, sexual violence and depravity like few have ever witnessed. Erotophonophilia, autassassinophilia, biastophilia-a deadly trio of paraphilias where normality does not apply and desire is synonymous with death. Some victims are more willing than others . . .

"Doug Brunell is back with his most traumatic work yet . . . *Black Devil Spine* is the most frightening thing I've ever read and puts even the most violent horror movie to shame . . . This is a horror novel like no other and is a journey of discovery to the darkest depths of the depraved soul rather than a novel that can be 'enjoyed' in the traditional sense. You have been warned!" -- HorrorCultFilms.com

HUMBOLDT FLEISCHHAUS - "It eats souls."

It starts deep in the forest. A brutal act of murder by townspeople disgusted at what has gone on behind closed doors.

"I beg you. Don't go down this road."

Over a hundred years later, the ancestors of those murderous townspeople will discover what happens when they are made responsible for past crimes. They will experience justice of the worst sort.

"I am the One. The Wicked Woman of the Woods."

The warnings are there. The sacrifices are being made. All that is needed is one tiny spark.

"It *hungers.*"

Stay far away from the Humboldt Fleischhaus.

"Brunell is slowly creating a version of the Pacific North Coast that rivals what Stephen King has done with the Eastern Seaboard - a vision of the world that is dark and terrible, and probably exactly what you should read next." -- Amazon review

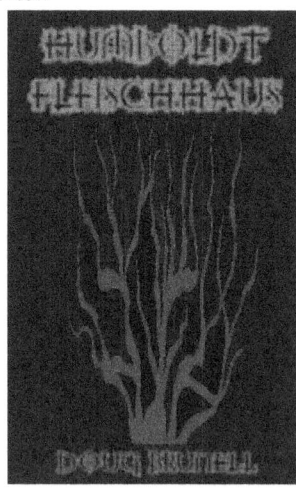

136

Sinful Cinema Series

THE ABDUCTORS - Nubile young cheerleaders! Sex slavers! Nudity! Bondage! Guns! Kidnapping! Torture! Sexual assault! Disney!

Plus: Anti-abortion terrorism, prostitutes, an infamous porn star, and an exclusive interview with Jeramie Rain (*The Last House on the Left*)!

This is a critical look at the 1972 grindhouse movie *The Abductors*, which helped set the standard for the strong female "secret agent" film while at the same time being described as "sexist" and "anti-PC." Prepare yourself for a sleazy descent into the world of sexploitation, real-life terrorism and, yes, Disney. You may think you know the movie, but you'll never view it the same way again after reading this.

CRYPT OF THE LIVING DEAD - In 1973 the world was introduced to a film that was quite unlike any vampire movie before or since. While it acknowledged the legend of the bloodsucker and teased at the occult, it also wanted very little to do with either, making for a cinematic experience as confusing as it was captivating. Adding to its allure was a star who was the main suspect in a bizarre murder case that had ties to psychics and the JFK assassination, and a co-star who went on to produce some of Hollywood's most critically acclaimed and beloved films. This is . . . *Crypt of the Living Dead*!

DESTRUCTION KINGS - Inspired by *Bad Boys* and *The Monster Squad*, the hilarious and offensive *Destruction Kings* caused the director to have panic attacks, divided audiences, and starred a man in an ape mask and a white guy in a Don King wig. And let's not forget John Stamos and Bill Cosby! This examination of the film also includes exclusive interviews with director/star/writer Chris Seaver, Ariauna Albright, and several others. Prepare to be amazed . . .

LAURE - It was to be the motion picture that captured the public's attention much the same way the *Emmanuelle* film had done, and it would do so by being written and directed by the author of the *Emmanuelle* novel. What moviegoers received, however, was a film directed by a French diplomat "sex maniac" who hid his identity from the world as he preached his sexual philosophy. This is the story of *Laure*, an erotic cinematic adventure of distinct and taboo pleasures, deceit, and an initial leading lady (Linda Lovelace) who refused to do nude scenes.

THE AMAZING MR. X - A film *noir* saddled with an unfortunate title. A leading lady who dies mysteriously before the film begins shooting. A director who would earn the wrath of the House of Unamerican Activities. The Turkish Delight and the Other Woman. This is the story behind *The Amazing Mr. X*, a film as much a product of its time as it was ahead of its time. A film that toys with audience expectations and makes lighting a character all its own. Prepare yourself as the worlds of horror and *noir* crime collide in a tale right out of Hollywood.

BEAST FROM HAUNTED CAVE - A film star related to a world-famous crooner. A female lead with a mysterious life. An actor who would later kill himself in the most grisly of ways. A future soap star who would be arrested for tax evasion and later lose his fortune after becoming obsessed with a collectible toy. A screenwriter and director who would both later influence one of cinema's most hailed directors. All of these people came together to make a strange heist/monster movie that could only come from the minds of the Corman brothers. Plus, exclusive interviews with filmmakers Darrell Draeger and Gary Wray!

"You're going to get weird, obscure and wacky cinema, which is just fine." - - Brian Harris, *Weng's Chop*

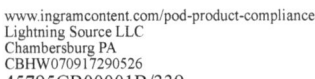